Home Ice

Home Ice

*Reflections on Backyard Rinks
and Frozen Ponds*

by Jack Falla

TAMPA, FLORIDA

Library of Congress Cataloging-in-Publication Data

Falla, Jack, 1944-
    Home ice : reflections on backyard rinks and frozen ponds / by Jack Falla.
        p. cm.
    ISBN 0-9653846-2-4
      1. Falla, Jack, 1944- 2. Skating rinks. 3. Hockey. 4. Ice skating.
I. Title.
   GV850.7 .F24 2000
   796.91—dc21

00-055902

Interior design and typesetting by Sue Knopf, Graffolio.

Published by McGregor Publishing, Inc., Tampa, Florida.
Printed and bound in Spain.

He acts it as life,
before he apprehends it as truth.

RALPH WALDO EMERSON

*To the former Barbara Spelman Baldwin
of Northampton, Massachusetts, for her gritty work
in the corners of our rink and our life.*

*And to everyone who has skated
at the Bacon Street Omni,
but especially to those who also shoveled.*

Contents

Foreword

When I started reading the manuscript for *Home Ice,* what I first liked about it is that it celebrates parts of the game that are rarely written about — backyard rinks, black ice, pickup hockey. The real roots of the game.

But *Home Ice,* touches on something else, too. Friendships. Relationships. The connections between and among people that somehow the game creates, strengthens and often preserves long past the day when sticks and skates are put away.

Home Ice isn't another sports celebrity biography or a book about tactics, strategies, statistics or behind-the-scenes wheelings and dealings. It's a book about the heart and soul of hockey — a backyard rink, a frozen pond and the families and friends who play on them.

It's wonderful how ice can be so warm.

BOBBY ORR
BOSTON, MASSACHUSETTS
MAY 23, 2000

Preface

'TO LOVE WINTER . . .'

In each of the last seventeen years — from my late thirties until well into my middle age — I have built a skating rink in the backyard of my home in Natick, Massachusetts. The reason I do this was best put by my wife Barbara about fourteen or fifteen years ago. It was a bitterly cold day during school vacation and Barbara and I were on the ice playing hockey with our son Brian and a few of his friends, one of whom was whining incessantly about the cold, repeating a chattering litany of, "It's so cold. I'm so f-f-reezing. I wish we could skate here in summer." To which Barbara, exasperated, finally said, "Matty, anyone can love summer, but to love winter you have to carry your sunshine around with you."

I don't think Matty — who has grown to exemplary adulthood and now brings his nephew to our rink — was either warmed or impressed. But I remembered Barbara's remark and repeated it many times in letters to friends because I'd never heard the rink's *raison d'être* phrased so lyrically.

In myriad and unexpected ways I hope soon to make clear, the rink lights our way through the long dark New England winters. It is a place for informal hockey games, large skating parties and solitary skates. It has been a lens through which I have watched my children and their friends grow up, a gateway into the lives of friends old and new, a bridge back to the frozen ponds and rinks of my childhood, and a kind of extra room where I sometimes go to exorcise life's demons and worries. I tend to think of my rink as the fictional Holly Golightly thought of Tiffany's—"[that] nothing very bad could happen to you there." And, give or take a high stick, nothing bad ever has.

But chiefly and always, our rink has been a bridge connecting me to the people I love.

All of which explains the rink, but not this book, the impetus for which came as much from without as within.

• • •

As my rink became increasingly important in my life I noticed that it also seemed to arouse more than a casual curiosity in others. Thus, in the spring of 1984, after I'd had the rink for two winters, I wrote an essay about it for *Sports Illustrated*. That piece ran on unnumbered pages in the back of the May 28, 1984, issue and was not listed in the magazine's table of contents. By coincidence, my six-page lead story on the Wayne Gretzky-led Edmonton Oilers wresting their first Stanley Cup from the four-time defending champion New York Islanders began on page twenty-eight of that same issue and was the first story listed in the table of contents. To my surprise the essay on the rink drew more reaction in the form of comments, calls and letters than did the story on the Stanley Cup. I was amazed at how many people, most of them middle-aged or older, had as children skated on makeshift rinks in backyards, vacant lots and farm fields and what memories and feelings those people still held for those ponds and rinks.

One of the readers was Don Wallace, then Executive Producer of *Hockey Night in Canada,* the popular Canadian

Broadcasting Corporation national telecast of NHL games. In 1985, Wallace produced a six-minute feature on my rink and televised it between periods of a mid-season game. The piece was well received and aired again during a 1985 play-off game.

Over the next few years I wrote four or five more essays on various facets of the rink, these appearing in the *The Hockey News* and its now defunct sister publication *Inside Hockey*. Those pieces, too, seemed to provoke a reader response deeper than and different from the one a writer might strike with a story on, say, fighting in the NHL or "What's Ray Bourque Really Like?" My pleasure in writing those rink stories and in readers' appreciation of them led me to think of writing a book about my family's rink, its place in our life, what I have learned from it and on it, and to what other rinks, ponds, people and memories it has led me.

But I think that writing a book is like having a child; that is, what's conceived in great ecstasy is often carried with a growing sense of burden and brought forth with some discomfort. Not being an enthusiast of discomfort — especially the scheduled discomfort of writing — I wrote not a word for more than a decade, until Barbara prodded me in the summer of 1999: "You really ought to get it all down on paper. We won't have the rink forever," she said.

The next morning I began writing *Home Ice*, at first reworking some earlier essays, but then quickly, to my surprise, heading off in new and unanticipated directions like a skater on open ice. I was surprised at where the writing took me—from Walter Gretzky's backyard to the ponds of my childhood. And I was even more surprised at the people who seemed to spring up from my keyboard and to whom the rink and hockey have connected me; some, such as my parents, deceased; others, such as my grandson, barely over the threshold of life's beginning; still others playing hockey anywhere from youth leagues to the NHL.

As the pen began to lead the writer, what emerged was as much a story about relationships and about the culture and nature of skating and hockey as it was about a backyard rink. As Barbara might say, I hope these essays carry some winter sunshine to their readers. But mainly I hope that *Home Ice* provides for its readers what my rink has so long provided for me — joy, warmth and light.

Home Ice

Home Ice

I stabbed my rink on a warm morning in the false spring of that February. After the children left for school — children should not have to see such things — I took a sixteen-inch knife, walked to the southeast corner of the 60-by-35-foot skating rink in the backyard of my home in Natick, Massachusetts, and thrust the blade through a gap in the plywood boards, through a piece of canvas that had served to seal the seam, and into the plastic liner. A stream of cold water, the lifeblood of the rink, poured through the hole and into the garden

By mid-afternoon the pool of water that had once been the rink had drained enough so that my then-twelve-year-old son Brian and I could step on islands of exposed plastic out to where we could pick up the regulation-size (six-by-four-foot) goal. We carried the goal to its off-season location in front of the garage where it would be a target for tennis balls until December brought the ice again.

I might have drained the rink completely by piercing it in the southwest corner — the deepest part — except that putting a hole there would have defied what I long ago learned is, for rink builders, an immutable law of hydrodynamics. Namely, water seeking its own level will find it in your neighbor's yard.

I discovered this in the early 1960s when, in my first effort to build a rink, I let the garden hose run all night in my parents' yard. The next morning I found not a frozen pool but a river running through our lilac bushes and under our neighbor's grape arbor. My engineering failure was nothing compared to the diplomatic problem facing my family, our relationship with those particular neighbors being such that Wiffle Balls hit into their yard were declared automatic double plays. The summer after I'd flooded their yard we changed that rule to automatic side retired. My yard produced a generation of straightaway hitters but no skaters.

I didn't try to build a rink again until I was an adult with a home and children of my own.

When, as a boy, I had tried to build a rink, no one asked me why. It surprised me that on seeing an adult building a rink, most of my friends assumed they knew why. Obviously, I was trying to make my children better hockey players or figure skaters. I knew that wasn't true, but why *was* I building it? I decided it had to do with the reason I have several times walked off golf courses when the starter insisted that a friend and I join with two strangers to make up a foursome, and why I won't sign up for squash court time or stand in ski lift lines, though if I had a mountain in my yard I would surely ski. In matters of personal recreation and casual sport, I prefer to descend the ladder of sports evolution, moving away from organization and mass participation toward individuality and spontaneity. Or, as my daughter Tracey said when she was eight and my wife Barbara asked her if she wanted to sign up for skating classes: "No. I want to have my own fun, not somebody else's fun."

I build my rink for the fun of it. On my first try, in late November of 1982, I packed the snow from an early storm into walls two to three feet high. These were to be the boundaries of a small rink. At sundown, I turned on the hose and let the water run over the now cleared and frozen ground, filling the rink.

"Will that kill the grass?" Barbara asked.

"I hope so," I said. It didn't. At 2 A.M., just as the rink was almost full, the southwest wall gave way and water flooded a corner of my neighbor's yard. Mrs. Henriques doesn't deserve this, I thought, as I dragged the hose down the bulk-head into the cellar. For years Mrs. Henriques had congenially endured my children and their friends tramping through her yard in pursuit of fouled-off tennis balls, overthrown footballs and even a few plastic golf balls sliced off of the second tee of what used to be Brian's three-hole backyard golf course. All of which is part of the hazard of living next to what my friends call "The Bacon Street Omni."

"I hope it doesn't kill her grass," Barbara said at breakfast.

"I hope so, too," I said.

"Plastic," said my friend Gerry as he surveyed the damage later that day. "You need plastic to keep the water from eating through the snow."

Gerry drove me to a lumberyard where I paid $90 for a roll of six-mil clear plastic.

I repaired the snow walls, laid down the plastic liner and turned on the hose. The design might have worked except that the sudden arrival of warm weather kept the water from freezing and, in a few days, melted the walls, thus sluicing much of the water back into Mrs. Henriques' yard.

"Boards," Gerry said several days later as he stood watching me fold up the plastic. "Boards don't melt."

I told him I was already down ninety bucks and all I wanted was a backyard rink, not the Calgary Saddledome.

Back at the lumberyard, Gerry selected a bunch of two-by-fours and several sheets of eight-by-four-foot three-quarter-inch plywood, a dozen of which he ordered sawed into eight-by-two-foot sections. "The two-foot-high boards will hold the plastic in place," he said, "but you'll want the four-foot-high ones behind the net."

The net? At that point I didn't even have a net. I wrote a check for more than $300. Gerry helped me load the wood into my station wagon and unload it in my yard.

"Gotta go," he said. "Good luck."

My first job was to dig postholes into the now-thawed ground. I don't have a posthole digger, but in the garage I found a four-foot iron bar with a sharpened end. I used the bar to smash up the rocky soil so I could scoop it out with a spade. I was poised for a thrust with the bar when Brian, then ten, came home from school.

"You look like Queequeg," he said. "The harpoon guy in that movie.

I told him *Moby Dick* was also a pretty good book. He said he'd take my word for it and went in the house. To this day we call that iron bar Queequeg, though years later I learned it is properly called a spud.

Tracey came home minutes later. "How much water will this take?" she asked.

"A lot," I said.

"We learned in school there's going to be a water shortage. By the year 2000 people will be dying of thirst."

I had a feeling Brian and Tracey had given me votes of no confidence. But I kept thrusting Queequeg into the ground, scooping out the dirt and rocks and setting sections of board in place.

I was lifting a board into a hole when Barbara came home. Barbara is an understanding woman, athletic herself and gracefully patient where the family's interest in sports is concerned. But the rink tested even Barbara.

"He's really going for it this time, sports fans," she said in mocking imitation of my too-frequent efforts at sounding like a hyper sports announcer.

"We can save the boards from year to year," I said, betraying a guilt so intense that it had me answering a question she hadn't even asked yet. Of course, then she had to ask.

"How much did all this cost?"

"About four hundred," I said. "But it's going to work this time."

Old towels, rags, a cut-up pup tent and pieces of a wading pool liner served to fill the gaps between and under the boards. I pulled out the clothesline pole, which was in the middle of the rink, and put it in the garage. "Only until March," I told Barbara.

It wasn't until after Christmas that steady subfreezing weather returned to New England. I rolled out the plastic liner, stapled it to the boards, turned on the hose and tried again. This time it worked. Sort of.

The liner held, the water froze and, on a Sunday morning in January, Brian, Tracey and two of their friends clomped down the sixteen-foot plywood boardwalk I'd built between the porch and the rink, stepped over the boards and skated.

"He pulled it off, sports fans," said Barbara.

But when Barbara and I tried to skate, the added pressure forced water up from under the ice. It ran out from the boards across the surface of the rink. We had to leave the ice to the kids.

By the time the rink froze solidly enough to support adults, business had me on the road. And by the time I returned, a snowstorm and the effects of one of New England's warmest winters since records have been kept had combined to turn the rink into a pen of alternately freezing and thawing slush. However, the children had used it for a few weeks and I counted it at least a partial success.

Word travelled fast. A few days after the children had first skated, my younger brothers, Cliff and Patrick, showed up with a hockey goal. It was the same rusting iron frame that had sat in my father's driveway for twelve years while Cliff and Pat, both goalies, skated through youth and high school hockey.

"How long did this take you?" Pat asked when he got his first look at the rink.

"About twenty-five years," I said. "You wouldn't remember."

In late March, when most of the water had evaporated or

leaked through holes I'd made in the plastic, I pulled up the boards, stored them in the garage, filled in the postholes and used Queequeg to chop up what ice remained. I threw the chunks of ice in the garden and rolled up the plastic and left it for the rubbish collectors. The grass did not die.

The next season I was ready early.

By late November the boards were in place and a new roll of plastic ($109) sat on the porch awaiting the first hard freeze.

On a Sunday in mid-December the forecast was for bitter cold with a 40 percent chance of snow. Snow during the year's first freeze is one of the worst things that can happen to a rink owner. The snow will lie atop a coat of ice so thin you can't stand on it to shovel. I remember my father's friend Bernie telling me how he once tried to solve that problem on his backyard rink by making a homemade wooden scraper with a ten-foot handle to allow him to stand on his lawn and scrape the snow off the ice as it fell. "There I was, Bernie the Human Zamboni," he said.

But Brian said we should go for it, and I figured that was a particularly strong commitment because we were holding tickets to that night's Princeton-Boston College hockey game and Brian knew that making ice would be an all-night job.

"Forty percent chance it will snow," I said.

"Sixty percent chance it won't," he said.

We put the plastic in place, turned on the water just as the sun was setting, and drove to the local indoor rink for Brian's hockey practice. I gave away the tickets.

While Brian's team practiced, a player's father told me a

horror story about his efforts to build a backyard rink. The man, who owns a landscaping company, brought in a bull-dozer to level an area for a 100-by-50-foot rink. He ordered an expensive custom-made extra-wide sheet of plastic and brought in an electric pump to bring up water from a pond on the edge of his property. "I was going BIG-time," he said.

But the water was going back to the pond. "It kept leak-ing and I couldn't figure out why," he said. "Finally I called my brother in to help me find the leak. We sailed out onto the rink in an aluminum skiff at night looking for leaks with a flashlight. We finally figured out that the roots and broken rocks exposed by the bulldozing had ripped through the plastic in about a zillion places. I spent a thousand dollars and never got a rink."

"But you got a funny story," I said and told him about Bernie the Human Zamboni.

It was well after midnight when the water finally filled the rink. It still hadn't snowed, but looked like it was going to. I went to bed anyway, still smiling at the image of two men sailing an aluminum boat across a skating rink at night.

It didn't snow that night — "Told you," said Brian — and by morning the rink was covered with at least an inch of ice. By Tuesday the children could skate on it, and by Thursday it was frozen solid. We all skated and Barbara and I played as a team in a pickup game against some of the neighbor-hood kids. I had played pond hockey with Barbara but had never seen her go into the corner of a boarded rink. She went with stick high and mayhem in her heart.

I don't do corners.

At night, after supper, I'd resurface the rink. It's as easy and pleasant a job as I know. I start at the far end of the rink and work back toward the porch, sending a soft spray of water from the garden hose across the surface of the freshly scraped ice. The water spreads like liquid wax, covering skate blade marks, flushing and sealing gouges and leaving the ice smooth, gray and inviting. I took pride in being rink architect, engineer and Chief Executive Ice Maker.

One night, after I'd resurfaced, Tracey turned on the back-yard light (then a 150-watt bulb set atop a fencepost; today five 150-watt floodlights are mounted on the roof and garage) and asked me to move a stereo speaker onto the back porch. She said she was going skating and handed me cassettes of albums by Michael Jackson, the Police and Def Leppard. "I won't play Def Leppard," I said, instantly feeling old and stupid. I put on the Michael Jackson album and went to the cellar for my skates.

Barbara, Brian, our neighbors and several neighborhood children joined us that night for nearly two hours of skating, interrupted, for me, only by the necessity of crawling on hands and knees through the house to change cassettes. I didn't want to waste time taking off my skates.

"You finally did it," said Mrs. Henriques, who had come out to walk her dog. She seemed genuinely happy for me. I wondered if Mrs. Henriques liked Michael Jackson.

Our neighbors were, or politely pretended to be, suitably awed by the rink. I politely pretended to be humble. "Just a little slap-together," I said.

"He's never been so proud of anything," said Barbara.

Late that night I still had my skates on and was scraping the ice while listening to an oldies radio station (I had grown tired of crawling in to change the tapes) when my friend Doc showed up, skates and hockey stick in hand and a six-pack of Molson beer under his arm.

We stuck the beers in a snowbank and wedged the bottle opener into a gap in the boards. "I knew you'd build a rink and forget to attach a beer opener to the boards," said Doc.

We passed the puck and snapped shots into the empty net. When Chuck Berry's *Johnny B. Goode* came on the radio, Doc did his Berry imitation, duck-walking (duck-skating?) around the rink, using his hockey stick as a guitar and lip syncing the words. Ice brings out the best in Doc.

Brian came out of the cellar with full goalie equipment on and said we could shoot at him for a while, no doubt because his other option was going to bed. We willingly blasted away, the pucks rising out of the dim light.

"Can you see those?" Doc asked.

"Not really, but it's a great angle drill," said Brian. "Either the puck hits you or it goes in the net.

Brian left after Doc and I started taking slap shots out of the dark shadows alongside the boards where a goalie couldn't even take his positioning cue from the angle of the stickblade.

"You two are sick," Brian said.

Doc and I stayed out another hour, skating, shooting and taking long pulls of beer.

"Have you ever been unhappy skating?" Doc asked me as we picked up the empties and headed for the porch.

I said I never had been.

I thought Barbara was still awake when I went to bed. "Have you ever been unhappy skating?" I asked her. But she must have been asleep because she didn't answer.

• • •

While a backyard swimming pool is generally if casually admired, a backyard rink seems to inspire a wider reaction — from open admiration to something even deeper: a desire to somehow be a part of the project. The latter feeling overcame my friend Steve Lockwood when he got his first look at the latest addition to the Bacon Street Omni.

Steve, a New Englander by birth and inclination, had returned that winter after four years in Los Angeles. He was in the process of opening an art studio in nearby Cambridge and had heard about my rink through mutual friends. On a drizzly afternoon a few days after Christmas, Steve's 139,000-mile Chevy pickup rattled into my driveway.

"Got a present for the rink," said Steve, who plays enough hockey to characterize himself as "a pretty intense blade man."

We walked through the house and onto the back porch.

"Oh, man, awesome effort," he said, opening the porch door, walking out into the rain and, I sensed, slipping into some sort of gonzo Southern California mode.

"You could get an NHL franchise with this thing," he said. "We add a dome, a few bleachers, the owner's luxury box over the porch." He looked at what little of my yard wasn't covered by the rink. "Parking could be a problem."

I told him that in future years I planned to make the rink longer by laying it out over the garden. He said I could make it wider if I cut down the large evergreen tree near the garage.

"The tree stays," said Barbara.

"Then nuke the garage," said Steve.

"And a logo," he said. "You need a logo on the ice. 'The Bacon Street Omni' in big letters, gray to match the house."

I laughed. But not as hard as I did about a month later when Steve mailed me nine designs for a center-ice logo and camera-ready artwork for stationery with the letterhead reading "The Bacon Street Omni" and a two-color logo. The stationery listed me as Owner, President, Rink Manager, Director of Player Personnel and six other titles. I never ordered the stationery, but I later used the design to make two dozen tee shirts.

We walked to Steve's truck. In the back he had a two-by-three-foot sheet of plywood on which he had done a full-color painting of the label of my favorite Canadian ale, Molson Golden.

"That's to hang on your boards," he said. "I gave it two coats of varnish so you can wipe off the puck marks. This is an industrial-strength sign, man."

I told Steve it would make its debut New Year's Day at the first annual Molson Cup tournament. In a way, the Molson Cup represents what the rink is all about.

The invitation, neatly typed on my father's business letterhead, arrived in late November. "We are pleased to inform you that you have been selected by our tournament committee to participate in the first annual Challenge Series at the Bacon Street Omni . . . ."

It was signed by my brothers and was a challenge to a two-on-two half-ice hockey game — Brian and me against them.

I replied via Special Delivery and in pidgin French:

"Club De Hockey de Rue Bacon accepter avec plaisir . . . ."

They arrived New Year's Day with the trophy in the back of Cliff's van. It was an empty aluminum beer keg with one of their old peewee hockey trophies mounted on top.

"If you win you have to display this in your living room for a year," said Cliff. "And right here," he pointed to the keg's equator of white enamel paint, "we're going to put the year and the names of the winners. Just like the Stanley Cup."

We used two plastic trash barrels for a goalie with the team on defense having the prerogative of arranging the barrels in the goalmouth any way it chose. We played two-on-two, changing from offense to defense after a goal was scored or when the defensive team cleared the puck by shooting it the length of the rink. It was a best-of-five series with a win going to the first team to score ten goals. That was it. There were no other rules. The game belonged — as all games should — to the people playing it. There were no triplicate parents' release forms to sign, no uniforms, no bending under the yoke of stripe-shirted authority. Justice was built in, not added on.

When Brian tripped Patrick, Bri was adjudged (at least by Patrick) to have exceeded the bounds of good sense and the limits of Pat's avuncular goodwill. On a later rush, Patrick checked Brian into the branch of an evergreen that hangs over the rink on the west side. "Child abuse," yelled Brian, picking himself up off the ice and watching Patrick score.

"That," yelled Patrick, "is what the fans came to see."

There were, of course, no fans and it didn't matter.

Brian and I lost 10-3, 10-6, 10-7. With the score 9-7 in the last game I willfully violated an unspoken rule about no high slap shots (none of us except Brian wore pads above the waist) and slapped the puck past Cliff. The puck hit the cross bar, bounced high into the air and came down in Mrs. Henriques' yard. "You want to go get it?" said Cliff. "We'll wait."

After Cliff and Pat won they insisted on an award ceremony complete with portions of "The Star-Spangled Banner" from a Rolling Stones concert album. Barbara took photos as they carried the beer keg around the rink, passing it from one to the other à la the Stanley Cup. A man walking down Bacon Street looked over and saw us. "Film at eleven," yelled Pat.

Before my brothers went home we resolved to expand the tournament in future years. "With a big party at the end," said Pat.

We used the rink for five more weeks. The only problem I had was fairly dividing hockey and figure skating schedules. I finally settled on a system that divided the post-school afternoon into two 75-minute sessions with hockey players and figure skaters alternating every other day as to which had first ice. Between sessions there was a 15-minute break for me to scrape the ice. Jack the Human Zamboni, I thought.

I took a lot of my ice time in the morning, skating by myself, a Beach Boys tape on the stereo.

Even after I'd stuck the rink with the knife, snow and rainwater covered it for so much of the time that it was mid-March before Barbara and I could pull the plastic off grass that had already started to turn green. She grabbed one corner of the plastic and I the other. Walking along the outside of the boards, we peeled it back like a bed sheet. When we got all the plastic to the south end of the rink, rainwater and melted ice had collected in a kind of long bubble. I drove Queequeg through the bubble, letting the water escape back into the grass. I put the clothesline pole back in.

"How sad," said Barbara.

Shots in the Dark

I understand it better now, but on the February morning when I was ten I remember thinking it was odd, probably irreverent — maybe even *sinful* — to be shooting a puck against a wall a few hours after my mother had died.

My mother lost what journalists tend to call "a long battle with cancer." I thought of it more as a street fight — no rounds, no rules, no draws and nobody to break it up. I thought she may have had the better of the kicking and scratching when she came home for Christmas and stayed with us until mid-January before going back to the hospital. But then came the phone call at about four in the morning and the visit from my aunt — my mother's sister — to my room.

I was saddened by my loss, angry about my mother losing. As the rest of the morning disintegrated into a chaos of doorbells and phone calls, I escaped to the backyard.

It was bitterly cold and I noticed a small frozen puddle a few feet in front of the garage wall. Water had collected in a depression my friends and I had made by wearing away the turf in our touch football games. My parents didn't mind some of my friends wearing cleats in the yard. I remember a friend's mother asking my mother rather archly, as I would later learn some well-off suburban women like to talk, "You let these kids tear up your yard like that?"

"That's what we bought it for," my mother said.

I wandered into the garage and found my hockey stick — its straight blade held together by layers of black friction tape — and a puck encrusted with the calcified dirt of some now forgotten driveway hockey game. I dropped the puck on the frozen puddle and started taking shots at the garage wall, toward an imaginary goal in front of which crouched an imaginary goalie. I didn't have much of a shot. Still don't. But I found intrinsic satisfaction and vague comfort in the act of shooting, of sweeping the puck forward and sending it where I wanted it to go. Whether I hit or missed, I controlled the stick, the puck and all the variables. If I did everything right, I could control the outcome of the act in a way that I could never control real life.

I don't know how many shots I took that morning. Probably not many before cold, obligation and guilt drove me back to the house. In the forty-plus years since, I've often gone outdoors to shoot pucks the way other people might go out to shoot basketballs. I do it for recreation and sometimes for escape.

Of course not all of my pucks have been pucks and not all of my goals have been goals. I've shot tennis balls, rolled-up socks, a wooden ball from a toy bowling game, rolls of tape, cans of tuna fish, Wiffle Balls, chunks of ice and pieces of wood. I've shot them at walls, closets, garage doors, beach chairs, bookcases and — my all-time favorite — a fireplace screen. Even today I cannot see a fireplace screen in even the most elegantly appointed living room without thinking — "top corner."

These days I have my own rink in my backyard and, on it, a regulation-size, steel-frame hockey goal. I shoot at it a lot in winter but, when the ice melts, I put the goal in the driveway for the kids. I rarely shoot at it there.

That goal sat in my driveway one August morning a few years ago when I was hit by what the late E. B. White of *The New Yorker* called "that end-of-summer-sadness our language has no word for." It was a sadness made worse by loneliness. My wife Barbara was visiting friends in New Orleans, our son Brian was at work earning money for his first year at boarding school, and our daughter Tracey was in Maine at a field hockey camp.

I ate breakfast alone and then went out to cut the grass. But when I got to the garage, I impulsively grabbed a hockey stick instead of the lawn mower. I took five pucks from a plastic milk case filled with pucks, dropped them on the driveway about twenty-five feet in front of the goal and began wristing them into the net. I remember two shots. One clanked into the goal off the crossbar. I automatically celebrated that one with an upraised stick. The other deflected off the right goal post and put a dent in my grill cover. You can't always make things happen the way you want them to.

What I remember best is that the act of shooting felt familiar. Comfortable. Steadying. But I'd taken only twenty shots or so when I started feeling self-conscious. What would our neighbors or a passerby think of seeing a grown man, alone, shooting hockey pucks at an empty net in what was shaping up as one of the hottest days of the summer?

I put my stick away and started the lawn mower. Neighbors understand lawn mowing. But, after more than forty years, I've come to understand something about shooting pucks. It is a good and blameless thing to do when the world fills with confusion and good-bye.

'Skate with Me,' She Said

Ice skating is part of my New England cultural heritage, which is an abstract way of saying that I learned early in life that a frozen pond is a good place to play hockey and to meet girls and, on days when you are very lucky, to do both.

Her approach was cool and direct. "Skate with me," she said, holding out a mittened hand.

I was fifteen and she was one of five girls my friends and I let into our Sunday afternoon pond hockey game. Our approach had been neither cool nor direct but calculated to strike a macho balance between cavalier and condescending. "Hey, you can use those extra sticks if you want to play," is what I think one of us said.

We played until it got too dark to see the puck. I was sitting on my goalie pads preparing to untie my skates when her hand came toward me. I took it and we skated to the middle of the pond. The bits of ice clinging to her white mitten melted in my bare hand, which was warm and steaming from having been in my goalie glove.

Maybe because I am a poor dancer but an adequate skater, ice is a social medium for me the way the hardwood of a dance floor is for others. As late as my senior year in college there was a girl I'd skate with on the pond in the Boston Public Garden in the late afternoon, the two of us gliding around almost in the shadow of the Ritz-Carlton Hotel, the horns of rush hour sounding around us.

In the winter before Barbara and I got married we used to skate together at the Boston College rink near her Brighton apartment. A few years later, when Barb and I bought a house with an uncommonly flat backyard, I put in our home-made skating rink. We are a winter people—or at least a winter family. Darkness and cold enliven us.

In the years we've had our rink it has become a kind of social pacemaker determining the pulse of our household in winter. It was often a mecca for our teenage children's raucous hockey games and skating parties, a peaceful place for my solitary early morning skates, a small self-contained world of laughter and hockey and hot chocolate. And although the day is long gone when Barbara and I could win a pickup hockey game against the neighborhood kids, she and I still play together sometimes in the evenings, skating under the floodlights, passing the puck and giving upraised stick salutes at goals scored into an empty net.

It was after one of those early evening skates during a school vacation — while then-seventeen-year-old Brian and fifteen-year-old Tracey were out for pizza with a group of their friends — that Barbara and I came in from the rink, pulled the cork from a well-aged cabernet sauvignon (winter isn't all hot chocolate), put on an album and sat down to a candlelight dinner.

How I wish I could tell you we were not listening to Johnny Mathis when they sprang upon us. Anyone but Mathis.

But it was too late.

Brian and five friends (two boys, three girls) fairly tumbled through the front door, while Tracey and three friends (one girl, two boys) came in the back. As soon as they heard Mathis they drilled us with a round of good-natured abuse.

"Head banging music," said one of Brian's friends.

"Cutting edge," said another.

"Rock the house," said Brian, pretending to smash an imaginary guitar over an imaginary amplifier.

They'd come back early to play hockey. Barbara and I, quickly caught up in the spirit of another impromptu hockey party, blew out the candles, snapped on the rink lights and headed to the cellar to bring up the extra skates we keep for kids who don't have or don't bring their own. Upstairs, Mathis gave way to hard rock pouring out of a boom box the size of a goalie pad.

With all ten kids equipped and on the ice, Barbara and I cleaned up the kitchen and went to bed. We did not go to sleep, because our bedroom is near the den, which is near the back porch, which is where the driving guitars of U-2 were rocking the night.

Barbara asked me to close the den door so we could get some sleep.

I got up to do that and, as I reached into the den to grab the doorknob, I looked out the den window and saw that the hockey game had stopped and a certain informal pairing off was taking place. A girl and boy sat on the boards talking. Another couple sat on the bench we keep on the back porch. Others passed a puck around.

One girl stood on the ice with her back to the house. A boy who was well-known to me skated toward her and, upon reaching her, put a hand on her hip and swung himself around as one might swing on a lamppost. Then he stopped beside her. They looked comfortable with each other. Easy. Natural. She slipped an arm around his waist and rested a white mittened hand on his hip.

I closed the door and went to bed.

First Ice

Today I test the season's first ice by putting one leg over the low boards of my backyard rink and gingerly shifting my weight from ground to ice until the ice either cracks or supports me. But years ago the testing of the season's first ice was a longer, more memorable and more dangerous process. . . .

• • •

I folded Mrs. Saltmarsh's *Boston Globe,* last of the fifty-two morning papers I delivered, by tucking the right-hand edge into the center section of the left-hand edge then giving it an authoritative thwack over my knee, setting it in that tubular shape that makes a newspaper easy to throw. A newspaper not thwacked over a knee was a newspaper that would explode in flight like a shotgunned duck, leaving the paperboy picking pages out of the shrubbery and off of the lawn.

It was then, standing at the bottom of two flights of stone stairs, that I had to make a decision: carry the paper up the stairs and flip it onto Mrs. Saltmarsh's porch; or try the toughest shot on the Winchester, Massachusetts, East Side No. 2 paper route — a prodigious underhand throw over the first flight of stairs, low enough to get under a rose arbor arching over the cement landing, yet with enough speed and elevation to carry the second flight of stairs, but not so much backspin that it would kick back off the porch.

Hand delivery was the percentage move. From January to November I trudged up those two flights of narrow, crooked stairs and plopped the paper on the doormat. But not in December. Or at least not always. There were cold mid-December mornings when, in order to save a few seconds, I eagerly attempted and often made "The Throw." These were dawns following cold, clear, often windless nights when the shallow waters of Long Pond may have frozen to a thickness sufficient to support a hockey game. Or they may not have. Which is why I had to hustle around my paper route about fifteen minutes faster than normal. I needed the extra time to check the ice, and a trip up Mrs. Saltmarsh's crumbling stairs would have consumed precious seconds.

Checking the ice was not a mission to be taken lightly. Friends at school awaited my verdict. The writing of term papers and honoring of piano lesson appointments hinged in large measure on whether or not we could play hockey on Long Pond that afternoon. We had our priorities.

It was axiomatic among us that neither the town Fire, Police nor Recreation departments would pronounce any natural ice safe to skate on unless it was thick enough to support the combined tonnage of the U.S. Seventh Fleet. As for our parents, they thought the ice hadn't been safe since the glaciers retreated. Our youthful standards were considerably more elastic. Besides, Long Pond was the shallowest body of water in town and anyone falling in would probably strangle in weeds before he drowned.

In Massachusetts the sun comes up at about seven o'clock in mid-December and I could see the day's first light peeking over the horizon from the top of a hill on the wooded path to the pond. That hill is part of a legally protected forest called the Middlesex Fells Reservation, which includes parts of the towns of Winchester, Stoneham and Medford. It is tempting now to rhapsodize about the beauty of those late-autumn sunrises, the shafts of heatless light shining through the oaks and pines and sparkling off the frost on fallen leaves. But in those days, I thought only of getting to the pond quickly and would have as gladly travelled that path had it been two-lane blacktop under neon lights.

Long Pond lies about one-third of a mile into the woods. It is shaped like a mitten with the thumb jutting out as a cove on the south side. The waters of the cove are shallow and well-shaded, and as Henry David Thoreau — who did his skating in nearby Concord — reported of Walden Pond, "[the water] skimmed over in the shadiest and shallowest coves, some days or even weeks before the general freezing."

I checked the cove first, walking a quarter of the way around the pond, my elongated morning shadow being first out on whatever ice there was. (Warning: Do not skate on ice that will not support your shadow.)

Whereas I visited the pond on even the slightest chance of its being frozen, I often found it covered by a skim of ice so thin as to be melted by noon. I reported this at school, amending my expert prediction — "three or four more days" — with the portentous certainty of an oracle.

At the time, I thought the freezing of a pond was simply a function of air temperature. It puzzled me how, after a particularly cold night in late November, there would sometimes be no ice at all, while the morning following a mid- or late-December night of lesser cold I might find the pond's surface completely frozen. I could have saved myself a few walks in the woods had I known that the freezing of a pond has as much to do with the properties of water as with the temperature of air.

Pond water must cool to thirty-seven degrees — molecularly speaking, that's the heaviest water can get — before it begins the freezing process. What happens on those first cold nights is that the air cools the surface water and, cold water being heavier than warm, the surface water sinks and is replaced by rising warmer water which, in turn, is cooled and sinks, the cycle continuing until all the water hits the magic number — thirty-seven. Now, instead of the surface water sinking, it remains concentrated at the top of the pond where, on a night when the temperature hits thirty-two or below, the water turns to ice. The shallower the pond, the less water to cool and the quicker the freeze. But a frozen pond is not necessarily a pond on which to play hockey. Thus, my inspection.

Preoccupied as I may have been, my first sight of the pond each fall was particularly pleasant in much the same way as is the first sight of the beach in summer. Chances were that I had not seen the pond since we'd played hockey on it the preceding February. Back then we had been skating on soft, white, rutted "snow ice." Now, early in the season, the pond would be covered with the prized "black ice," which, as Thoreau described it, is "interesting and perfect, being hard, dark and transparent." Black ice is ideal for the nearly effortless glidings of skaters and for the flat, unimpeded skimming of a puck.

Black ice also affords an excellent view of the bottom of a pond; the seeming proximity to submerged weeds and rocks gives the impression of the ice being thinner than it is. Snow ice, on the other hand, poses the danger of never allowing you to know how thick — or thin — it is.

I tested the Long Pond ice by butt-ending it with the thick end of a dead branch. If I broke through, I'd take an approximate measure of the thickness. Statistics like that added credibility to the school report. If I couldn't break through then I moved on to the rock test.

I selected a handful of rocks from the shore and threw them in high arcs, intending for them to hit the ice at progressively greater distances. Sometimes the rocks would ply through the ice far from shore. But, if it was to be a skating day, all the rocks would hit the ice and skitter away, making a a high sharp *twaaaaaaaang* like the sound of breaking guitar strings, the echo carrying to the boulders on the far shore.

Those huge flat-sided rocks jutting out here and there around the north shore were among the reasons Long Pond was ideal for hockey. If there is one thing you cannot do on most ponds it is shoot a puck. Try it and the puck will either skid up on shore where you won't be able to retrieve it without ruining the sharpening job on your skates or, if you're on a lake or a big pond, your shot — if it doesn't hit a goal, a goalie or a skater — will sail so far it will be dark by the time you retrieve it. But those boulders on Long Pond gave us natural backstops on which to practice our shots. It is not coincidental, I think, that a lot of National Hockey League old timers and some older college coaches say that one of the chief differences between players of the last two generations is that, for the last twenty-five years or so, almost every player has had a hard shot, whereas before the 1970s Bobby Orr-inspired hockey rink boom, only a few players on each team — Bernie "Boom Boom" Geoffrion of the 1950s Montreal Canadiens and Bobby and Dennis Hull of the 1960s Chicago Blackhawks come to mind — had big, heavy shots. It seems reasonable to trace the recent proliferation of firepower to the ascendancy of a generation that played virtually all of its hockey on indoor rinks where high boards topped by shatter-proof glass formed all-encompassing backstops. Pond hockey, on the other hand, demands and rewards stickhandling skills, perhaps the one facet of today's dump-and-chase game where proficiency is wanting on even the highest levels. But I digress.

If sticks and stones did not break the ice, there was one more test to try. If I could walk on the ice there would be hockey that afternoon. But one does not stroll cavalierly onto new ice. I first put one foot on the ice and gradually transferred my weight onto it. If the ice held, then I would bring my other foot onto it and begin shuffling away from the shore.

While town officials were loath to affix their *nihil obstat* to early-season ice, I took it as a form of implied consent that red-and-white lifesaving rings and ladders were affixed to stands at various points around the pond. My friends and I found the ladders useful as backstops. We often played "no lifting" games and, while those ladders never saved a life that I know of, they saved more pucks than Dominik Hasek.

The lifesaving rings were a different story. We never figured out any practical use for them and did not think the pond was deep enough to require flotation devices. Of course, as with all ponds everywhere, there were a couple of places in the middle where we couldn't see bottom, and the younger kids prattled on about a "bottomless pit" no doubt harboring giant snapping turtles and The Long Pond Monster. I think those places were simply too far from shore for dead leaves to accumulate. Nevertheless, we seldom played early-season hockey in the middle of the pond.

• • •

One frigid December morning when there seemed to be particularly thick black ice, I skipped the branch and rock tests and didn't even bother shuffling onto the ice. Instead, I walked out on a fallen tree so I could test the thickness of the ice about six feet from shore. I stood on the dead limb and — for security's sake — reached up and grabbed the overhanging branches of a tree growing close to shore. I held those branches with my right hand while gingerly placing my left foot on the ice. The ice held. I transferred yet a little more weight onto my left foot. The ice still held. Now, grasping the overhead branches and probably looking like a subway commuter hanging onto to a ceiling rail, I confidently put both feet on the ice. The ice held. I bounced my weight once. The ice broke.

The branch I was foolishly holding onto bent like a fishing pole and I was quickly lowered into the water. The water was cold but not deep. The mud was deep. Decades worth of decomposing leaf mush squished into my shoes. Reeking muck and rotting weeds swirled around my blue jeans. I let go of the betraying branch and used my hands to hoist myself back onto the fallen tree. I was wet to mid-thigh and covered with the vilest smelling mud this side of a compost pile. It was in that condition that I walked home, skulking along stiff-legged, my empty *Boston Globe* bag over my shoulder; I probably looked like a bedraggled vagabond to the early morning commuters who saw me walk out of the woods onto Highland Avenue.

Washed, changed and otherwise recovered, I went to school, where — with my usual affectations of aplomb and expertise — I pronounced the ice unfit for another day or two. I mentioned nothing of having fallen in. An oracle's credibility is a fragile thing and, once damaged, can never be wholly recovered.

It was later that week, when the ice finally froze thick and solid, that my friends and I met at the pond for the season's first hockey game. The fallen tree upon which I had stood formed a convenient natural bench where we could sit and put on our skates. Two or three of us were sitting there when someone noticed the irregular pattern of ice chunks frozen together.

"Looks like someone fell in," he said.

"Looks like," I said.

We played hockey all afternoon and into the early evening. It was dark when we came down the hill near Mrs. Saltmarsh's house with the lights of the town shining below us and Orion rising high in the sky.

Last Ice

I have gone from matador to picador. Instead of draining my rink quickly with a single knife thrust at the deep end as I used to do, I now drain it slowly by repeatedly jabbing the plastic liner with a dandelion picker. When a rising March sun softens the ice at the north end of the rink, I take the dandelion picker — a three-foot wooden shaft tipped by a metal rod with a notched end — and poke ten or a dozen jagged holes in the liner at the shallow end of the rink. The holes let the meltwater seep slowly into the ground. As the water recedes I can walk on the exposed plastic and poke a few more holes farther out so that, over a period of days, the rink waters recede like an outgoing tide. It takes longer, but it's better than sending rivulets of muddy water into my neighbor's yard.

I got greedy in 1997 and, wading out into the water one afternoon, I poked what must have been fifty or sixty holes in the plastic. In the space of six hours I went from having a skating rink in my yard to having a wading pool in my cellar as the rink water, draining into already rain-saturated ground, seeped into my bulkhead and under the cellar door. I take it slower now.

Once the rink is drained, I begin the dolorous job of removing the plastic and pulling up the boards. It's the gloomiest job in the gloomiest month, but it taxes my back more than my brain and leaves me time to think. What I think about most often is that I would have saved myself a lot of work if I'd listened to Brian a few years ago when he came up with a scheme for leaving the rink boards in place year-round. "Arena football," he said. But permanent boards — two of them adorned with the rink's name, *The Bacon Street Omni*, in bright red letters — would look out of place in summer and spoil a perfectly serviceable volleyball court, Wiffle Ball field and golf pitching range. So I go about my sad and solitary business.

In many ways our rink is like our Christmas tree, going up in late fall amidst much jollity and with the help of many willing hands, but coming down only when I reluctantly take it down myself, burdened with that unspeakable end-of-the-holidays sadness.

I must have looked particularly morose a couple of years ago as I sliced the huge plastic liner into strips to be rolled, tied and stacked like firewood on the patio pending their removal. I'd stripped away about half the plastic when Barbara came out of the house, stepped onto the now grassy surface of the iceless rink, and began a simulated skate across the grass, moving with a long exaggerated stride, her body bent sharply forward and her hands folded behind her back so that she looked like a skater in a Frans Hals paint-ing. "I'm in denial," she said as she did a neatly executed crossover stride and "skated" back to the house. In two decades that's the only time I can remember laughing while taking down the rink.

That day I continued slicing and rolling until I came to the last few feet of plastic which were, as usual, under a foot-thick reef of ice where the south end of the rink is protected by four-foot-high boards that block the rays of the equinoxial sun. I broke up the ice with a sledge hammer and tossed the chunks of clear ice into the garden. Say this for a backyard rink: it keeps you in touch with the irreducible realities of skating — ice and cold. And yet those realities, if not being reduced, are in some sense being replaced or altered. I wonder how many kids who have skated only on artificial ice, or couch potatoes whose only connection to ice is to see it on TV, or video game junkies who prefer pixels to pucks, know that natural ice is clear and not white like the painted ice they see on TV, in video games and in rinks. There's no dreadful consequence to that and yet it seems like another step away from the natural origins of our winter game. My rink reminds me I'm a hockey guy in a hockey family; cold and ice keep me out of the Barcalounger and away from video games.

But even ice is becoming superfluous now as the boom in roller hockey and in-line skating carries the joy of skating to people who live in places where there is no natural ice. And that's good. But there *is* a difference, as was demonstrated to me a few years ago when my friend Doc came to Boston from Houston, where he is headmaster of a private school.

"I've got a meeting in Boston on March 4. You gonna have ice?" Doc asked when he phoned in mid-February.

"Cliffhanger. The line on ice in March is 6-5 pick 'em," I said.

"I'm bringing my skates," he said. "You'd better have ice."

He lucked out. March 4 was the second to last day we had skateable ice. Doc hadn't skated on natural ice since he and his family had left New England ten years earlier. But before that he was a hockey maniac, often playing on the lakes and ponds of his native Wellesley, Massachusetts, and later routinely getting into the Saturday pickup games on Nonesuch Pond a few yards from his first home in Natick, Massachusetts. (Doc was so hard-core that he once talked me into playing hockey on Nonesuch Pond by the light of a full moon. It was surreal, eerie and wonderful until the ice cracked and we scrambled up the shore like the Marines landing on Iwo Jima.) But since moving first to Louisiana and then to Texas, Doc is on his third pair of in-line skates. It took him days just to find his hockey skates before his trip to Boston.

As he clomped down the wooden runway from my porch to the rink, skated a lap around the ice and took his first shot in a decade (clanking the puck off the crossbar and out of the rink), he slipped into his natural 1970s patois: "Ain't nothing like the real thing, baby," he said. I've seen a lot of happy people on my rink. And no sad ones. But I'm not sure I've ever seen one as happy as Doc, who, for the next half hour, skated, shot and stickhandled himself into a breathless frenzy before Barbara called us to dinner.

Ten days later I got a letter from Doc, who by that time had returned to Houston. "Rollerblading is fun," he wrote, "but it doesn't hold a candle to the magic of cruisin' on ice."

I'm glad I can domesticate that magic and keep it in my yard. But lately I wonder how much longer I can continue to do so. In recent years the rink has brought me face to disconcerting face with another irreducible reality of sport and of life — age. I was thirty-eight when I first built the rink. Back then I could put it up and take it down by myself. But I am fifty-five as I write this and, while social euphemism calls that "middle age," the grim actuarial reality is that if life were a golf course I'd be on the back nine.

I need help with the rink these days, help I'm often too proud to ask for (Ralph Waldo Emerson was right: the highest price you can pay for something is to ask for it). Columbus Day weekend used to be a kind of barn-raising, with Brian and his friends digging postholes and putting up about two-thirds of the boards while I was consigned to barbecuing chicken and keeping an adequate supply of beer on ice. But some of those guys have moved, some have married, some have other things to do. So now I start digging the postholes by myself in early October and hope I can finish before the general freeze-up in late November. It is late October as I write this and — for the first time in sixteen years — I have genuine doubts about whether I can beat the frost without making a few phone calls to friends who have offered to help. "Brian or Smitty would help you," Barb said last week. "Sometimes you just have to make a statement," I said. And today as I type out the words it seems a foolishly vain thing to have said. But digging remains easier than asking. (Note: I got the boards up with about a week to spare.)

I can still shovel the rink by myself, but it takes longer these days and instead of looking ahead at the snow I've yet to tie into, I more often find encouragement by looking back at the ice I've already cleared.

"Do you think we'll have the rink next year?" Barbara asked a few years ago as we went for the season's final skate on the Sunday morning after Doc left.

I knew what she was driving at. A season of record snow in the winter of 1993-94 and of record warmth over the next several years, including the 1997-98 year of El Niño, had steadily reduced the number of skating days. The guest book we ask everyone to sign when they skate for the first time in a season had shown dwindling numbers not only because of the warmth but because our own children and so many of their friends who used to use the rink had gone off to college. In 1990-91 we had seventy-two names in our book and a record seventy-three the following winter. But by the year of El Niño, only fifteen skaters used the rink, and this during a period of perhaps twelve days that were cold enough for skating. Worse, the warming weather and the wet, sticky ice-ruining snow it produces had put the skating-to-maintenance ratio at about three-to-one in favor of maintenance. Perhaps the rink, too, is on the back nine.

"We'll keep it for as long as we can," I said to Barb, though I privately wondered how long that can be. What I didn't say — and why we still have the rink — is that I want to hear more dingers off the crossbar, go for more solitary early morning skates, and maybe someday see our grandchild shuffling along the boards in that learning-to-skate awkwardness, outlined against the red sky of a late-winter afternoon, oblivious to the gathering darkness and strengthening cold.

Or am I in denial?

Black Ice, Emerson, and the Almost-Perfect Day

I sometimes ask friends for their descriptions of the perfect day and generally get answers involving Rome, Paris, beaches, music, vintage wines, gourmet food and various combinations of The Big Trifecta — love, romance and sex.

It's not that I have anything against Paris and Rome (except that they're not Boston and Montreal), but if you ask me to describe my perfect day, skating on black ice will be in the mix, though not to the exclusion of food, wine, music, and the Big Trifecta.

In our mid-summer conversations of how we might spend New Year's Eve 1999 — that over-hyped and synthetically jolly start to the next millennium — Barbara and I considered domestic and foreign travel. But what we ended up doing was staying home, eating a late-night dinner and going out on our backyard rink just before midnight to skate out of one century and into the next.

"Happy New Year," I said to Barb as we hit the ice at about five minutes before midnight. "You're early," said Barb, "Two-century offside."

We were glad to be in our own backyard and with each other and away from the forced and fraudulent joy of any organized first-night celebration. "The wise man stays home," wrote the New England Transcendentalist philosopher Ralph Waldo Emerson, himself a skater and a member of what has to be the all-time, all-star, all-literary line. Never did more immortal writing talent skate in one backyard than on Friday, November 25, 1841, when an early cold snap froze a flooded section of the orchard behind Emerson's Concord, Massachusetts, home, the "Old Manse." Visiting friends Nathaniel (*The House of the Seven Gables*) Hawthorne and Henry David (*Walden*) Thoreau joined Emerson for a brief skate that was chronicled by Hawthorne's wife Sophia, who watched it from an upstairs window. She described Thoreau, apparently the strongest skater, as taking "Bacchic leaps," while Hawthorne, wrapped in his cloak, skated "like a self-impelled Greek statue." Emerson was "evidently too weary to hold himself erect" and thus skated stooped over, "half-lying on the air," a skating posture, we should note, that never hurt Wayne Gretzky, who was something of a transcendentalist in his own right. It's a good thing Sophia Hawthorne wasn't a mnemonically inclined NHL flack, or Thoreau, Hawthorne and Emerson might have become "THE" line and the answer to a question on the Advanced Placement English Test.

Neither Barbara nor I took any Bacchic leaps (too tough on the groin) on New Year's Eve. We just skated around, sometimes holding hands, waiting for the twenty-first century to check in. Neither of us wore a watch, nor did we need one. At midnight we were surrounded by the muffled boom of fireworks far and near and the rising of a chorus of indistinguishable voices presumably cheering in the new century or cheering out the old. Or both. We wished each other a happy New Year and, after a few more minutes of skating, I said I was heading in. "Would you turn off the rink lights? I want to see the stars," Barb said. I took off my skates and walked to the garage to hit the switch controlling the four 150-watt floodlights mounted on the garage wall. "There's Gemini, the twins," said Barb as soon as the lights went out. She pointed to a constellation that looked to me like two cosmic defensemen. "And there's Orion," she said, pointing directly overhead. Orion is one of the few constellations I can identify and is the one whose passage across the heavens parallels the passage of the New England hockey season. In November, as I race with winter to put up my rink before the ground freezes, I see Orion rising in the southeast, a lumbering goalie hauling himself slowly, almost reluctantly, over the boards. By January, the heart of the hockey season, Orion is directly over our rink, a looming presence crouched at the top of some intergalactic crease. By spring and ice-out he has moved toward the southwest horizon, where it's easy for me to fancy him stumping off to the dressing room, though Barbara disagrees. "Where do you think he's going?" I once asked her.

"First tee," she said.

In 32 years of marriage we've tried New Year's Eves every way there is — home and away, big groups and small, sit-down dinner parties and milling stand-ups — and none were so memorable that they kept New Year's Eve from finishing anywhere but dead last when my friend Doc and I ranked the holidays a few years ago. Christmas Eve, Christmas and Thanksgiving — Anticipation, Fulfillment, and Gratitude — swept the gold, silver and bronze. The New Year's Eve Barb and I spent on our rink doesn't alter those standings. But it was better than any previous New Year's Eve.

I was cleaning up the kitchen when Barb came clomping in, careful to step on the small rugs we use to keep skate blades from cutting the kitchen floor tile. "Pretty close to the perfect day," she said, eyeing the remains of two lobsters and an empty bottle of Pouilly-Fuissé. The voices of Sarah Brightman and Andrea Bocelli singing *"Con Te Patiro"* poured from the stereo. "Music to load the dishwasher by?" asked Barb. I poured us small glasses of a tawny port and, as we attacked the kitchen together, we went over some of the better days of the year. The best day, clearly, was the birth day of our first grandchild. And there were a handful of other family milestones and achievements. But those were days that left their stamp on us. Of the days that *we* stamped — days on which we actively imprinted the joy rather than vice versa — I said, "I thought Wednesday was pretty great."

"It was the all-time skating day," she said. "Pretty good food day, too."

The Wednesday before New Year's Eve was the fourth in a series of cold days during which both our rink and nearby Little Jennings Pond had ice thick enough to support skating. Our rink logbook shows that December 29, 1999, marked the first time in four globally warming years that we were able to skate on our backyard rink before January. I took the first skate in the early morning, moving over ice so clear I could distinguish individual blades of grass and veins of maple leaves beneath the plastic liner. It was like skating on the crystal top of a coffee table, and my pleasure in the skating was enhanced by the wonder that such a seemingly fragile surface could hold me up. I stickhandled a de-fuzzed and frozen tennis ball — it was a little too early in the morning to be banging pucks off the boards — and took slapshots aimed at dotting the "I" in the big red "BACON ST. OMNI" sign painted on the high boards behind the net. I came close a couple of times before I got under a shot too much and sent the ball sailing over the boards and the wire fencing and out of the rink. But by then I was tired and sweating and getting the first stiffening of the shin splints that in my middle age seem to accompany the season's first skate. I came in to pour a cup of coffee and take it to my writing room where I was working on a magazine story. *Nulla dies sine linea* — not a day without a line, as some Latin writer once said. But for me it is not the writing but the *having written* that gives pleasure to the day.

Later in the morning Barbara went out on the rink. From the den window I could see her chugging around counterclockwise, swinging hand weights, her head bopping to the sound of whatever was on the headset she was wearing. "That's the best ice ever," she said when she came in.

It may well have been the best ice in the seventeen-year life of our rink, but even better ice lay ahead.

* * * *

By three o'clock that afternoon the sun was already slipping toward the horizon, my fifty-five-year-old knees were throbbing with the effects of my morning skate and I was having a hard job convincing myself to get up off the couch and check the ice at Little Jennings Pond. "I'm too old for double sessions," I muttered to Barb as I headed to the cellar to find my old hockey bag, the one with the rotting leather-palmed hockey gloves, stocking hat, old skate rag, pucks, spare laces and other hockey effluvia that hadn't seen the light of day since I'd tossed the bag down cellar at the end of last winter. I grabbed bag, skates, stick and car keys and drove the half mile to Little Jennings.

Strictly speaking, there is no "Little" Jennings Pond. Look on a map of Natick, Massachusetts, and the pond, formed by several streams running out of the town forest, will be identified simply as "Jennings." What I and other locals call "Little Jennings" is the small, shallow, marshy pond formed before the waters flow east through a culvert under Oak Street and spread into a much bigger pond — Jennings Pond Proper, as it were. The beauty of Little Jennings is that it freezes early and is so shallow that it's safer than other ponds and lakes. First ice always scares me a little, so I was glad to look out on the pond and see the hacked up white area of ice between two tree branches, obviously the site of a hockey game earlier in the day. A man and two boys — father and sons, I assumed — were taking off their skates on the shore as I cautiously shuffled a few feet onto the ice and plopped down my bag. "How's the ice?" I asked the man, which is remarkable only when you consider that I start conversations with strangers about as often as I get my name on the Stanley Cup. But ice is a kind of social connective tissue for me and I'm more outgoing and less guarded when I'm on it.

"It's great on this side but be careful over there," he said, pointing to the more distant of the two main streams that flow out of the forest, through the marsh and into the pond.

By the time I laced up my skates — always a cold, uncomfortable process outdoors and one a thirty-eight-inch waist does nothing to make easier — the boys and the man had gone and I had the pond to myself.

I slipped on my hockey gloves, an act that, on the face of it, made very little sense because there was no one there to slash me on the hands. But forty-plus years ago an older kid on another pond had told me, "Hockey gloves are good for chopping through the ice if you fall in." Made sense to me.

I tossed out a puck and began skating across the snowy ice that marked the site of the earlier hockey game and toward the black virgin ice beyond. I wasn't four strides onto the all-black ice before I lost my dribble and the puck slid off my stick. Amen, Amen I say unto ye, if ye would stick-handle on black ice, *bring a puck with a label.* I had only two pucks in my hockey bag and neither had a label. It's hard to see a black puck on black ice, so I swung back into the snowy hockey area between two logs that had obviously been used for goals. I skated this way and that, occasionally shooting the puck along the ice, banging it off one of the logs. It was after such a shot at the log farthest out on the pond, as I was swinging behind the makeshift goal ready to go back the other way, that I looked up and saw two teenage boys coming off the shore and onto the ice. Neither had skates. One boy, dressed only in a light denim jacket, stood on the ice and cuffed a cigarette while he bounced on the balls of his feet in an apparent effort to keep warm. The other boy wore a large parka, but not large enough to hide the fact that he was considerably overweight. He had the jowly face of an older man. He looked like a fourteen-year-old John Goodman.

As I stickhandled again around the west goal, the jowly boy walked out onto the ice, picked up the log marking the east goal and threw it toward the open water just in front of the culvert. The log slid along the ice and plopped softly into the water. It wasn't my log, nor was it something that couldn't be easily replaced, nor was it anything I was even using at the time, nor was the throwing of it into the water in any way directed at me. But that didn't matter. I strafed the kid anyway.

Swinging around the west goal again, picking up the puck and starting up ice, I skated close to The Smoker, then straight at Jowls, coming within a few feet of the latter before swinging the puck and myself around him as one would swing outside of a plastic cone in a skating drill. There was neither eye nor body contact, nor did I say anything or act in any way like Jowls was a human being and not a rock or a lily pad to be stickhandled around in one's normal recreational course. But it was a brushback nonetheless. Certainly nothing I'd try in a subway station or a parking lot, but on ice it's always different for me. And Emerson was right when he said skates are "fetters on land but wings on ice." I had the wings and I was inclined to use them.

By the time I'd circled the remaining goal and started back up ice for another strafing run, Jowls and The Smoker were already walking up the hill and back toward Oak Street. The brushback had worked. But I knew if I returned to the pond in several weeks and found the ice pocked with footprints and littered with sticks, cigarette butts and other detritus, the damage would most likely be the work of Jowls and The Smoker or others of their loutish tribe.

Abandoning the puck, I went for a long skate in the widest circle I dared to make, having regard for the possibly unsafe ice near the culvert and feeder stream. The sun had already slipped behind the hills of the town forest, leaving a tier of trees starkly outlined against the cold low-angled solstitial light. It was a memorable sunset, the more so because it had snuck up on me and was a backdrop for something I so much like to do. That old stooped-over skater Emerson was right again when he wrote that the moon or sunset we go out merely to gawk at is never as beautiful "as that which lights our necessary journey."

My skating may not have been completely necessary but dinner was, so I traded my skates for my now-freezing deck shoes, threw my stick and bag in the trunk and drove downtown to the local fishmonger's to pick up the ingredients for the six-fish *bouillabaisse* I'd promised to make for dinner.

When I got home, Barb was back out on the rink, without the handweights this time but still bopping to the music on the headset and moving with the choppy skating stride that hasn't smoothed out one whit in the thirty-two years I've known her. While she skated, I combined shrimp, mussels, scallops, lobster, swordfish, little neck clams and not illiberal quantities of wine, garlic and various spices, herbs and vegetables into the classic French fish stew.

The music to cook by was genuine French Cajun by the Louisiana group Beau Soleil. But when it was time to dine, Beau Soleil's *"L'amour ou La Folie"* gave way to Sinatra's "In the Wee Small Hours."

Barbara, hungry and flushed-faced from the cold, came in for dinner. The near-perfect day ended with the perfect evening.

Rink Rat Odyssey

He saw the townlands
And learned the minds of many men.

HOMER
THE ODYSSEY

Selling it was the hard part.

It's not that Barbara is intolerant of my pursuing odd and diverse interests in sport; she is, after all, the woman who brought me a mug of hot chocolate while I piled up snow to make a luge run from the peak of our garage after the Blizzard of '78. Nor was she unreasonable about Brian using her back flower garden as the finishing hole for his backyard golf course, notwithstanding that the only way to birdie the hole was to risk a wedge shot over the house. "Break a window, lose your tour card," was all she'd said about that.

But what I was proposing would take me away from the family for a week of Christmas school vacation, sacrosanct "family time" for Barbara; or, as Tracey put it in her chiding mimicry: "We will *all* go cross-country skiing and we will all *like* cross-country skiing."

I wanted to go cross-country driving. Alone. From our home in Natick, Massachusetts, through southern Ontario and Minnesota to visit three families who, like ours, had built hockey rinks in their backyards. The day after Christmas I tried explaining my idea to Barbara with what I thought was a deft bit of intellectual stickhandling: "Meeting these people and seeing their rinks will help me write about a little-known facet of northern recreational heritage," I said. Or something like that.

"Palaver," she said. Or something like that.

With pretentious rationalization high-sticked at the domestic blue line, I came back with my rarest and most dazzling move. I told the truth. "These people sound interesting. It's like we're all part of the same lunatic fringe," I said. "Besides. I have the week off."

Barb said I should take the station wagon because it has the best stereo and that, in a solo drive halfway across North America, "album selection is key."

The families I planned to visit in the winter of 1986-87 were:

- The Gretzkys of Brantford, Ontario, where father Walter was then using a lawn sprinkler to flood his backyard, thus creating the ice on which son Wayne first learned the moves that would make him the greatest scorer in hockey.
- Ronn Hartviksen of Thunder Bay, Ontario, who, besides being a recreational hockey player, is an artist who has developed a technique for painting on what he calls his "ice canvas," thus turning his rink into a medium of self-expression.

- The Fryberger family of Duluth, Minnesota, who maintained what is possibly the grandaddy of all United States backyard rinks: a flooded house lot that was then, and had been for more than forty years, a neighborhood fixture sending forth hockey players — including 1960 Olympic gold medalist Tommy Williams and 1980 gold medalist Phil Verchota — the way a frog pond sends forth tadpoles.

I'd heard of the Hartviksen and Fryberger rinks (everyone knew about the Gretzky rink) through a kind of freemasonry of backyard rink owners the ranks of which fellowship I'd unwittingly joined when I'd built my own rink and then written a story about it for *Sports Illustrated.* Thereupon followed a steady flow of letters, phone calls and visits from folks who had built rinks, were planning to build rinks, had failed in the attempt to build rinks or who merely wanted to reminisce about rinks they'd known in their youth. Clearly, backyard rinks have a way of insinuating themselves into people's lives and of holding on with a tenacity out of all proportion to their recreational worth. You build a rink because you want one; but you keep it because you come to need it. I wanted a closer look at that need.

I wanted to visit the Gretzkys first.

"This might be the last year Dad will have a rink," Wayne had told me in November of that year when he was in Boston for a game with the Bruins and I was covering that game as a writer. I thus saw my planned visit to Brantford as something of a pilgrimage, a chance to see — and to skate on —

this mecca of backyard rinks before it melted into hockey history. I also wanted to see Walter Gretzky again. The man once gave me a useful tip on combining the arts of rink maintenance and parenting. We were in Detroit's Joe Louis Arena in February 1984, he to watch Wayne and the Oilers play the Red Wings, I to research a magazine profile of Wayne.

My interview with Walter started badly. He spoke hesitantly, guardedly, about his son. It seemed obvious that he either didn't like or didn't trust reporters. But he seemed willing to ramble on animatedly about his backyard rink. In the interest of maintaining some kind of flow to the conversation, I junked my list of reporter's questions and we spent much of the game — albeit not when Wayne was on the ice — talking about our backyard rinks. I told him that one of the most vexing problems I faced was that my kids and their friends left hockey equipment strewn all over the ice when they came in at night, thus necessitating my picking up their gear before I could begin to resurface.

"Ohhhhh, Wayne and his brothers used to make me so mad doing that," Walter said. "So one night I just left it all out there and turned on the sprinkler. Froze it all in."

If you ever wonder how Wayne Gretzky turned out to be among the least spoiled of the world's athletic megastars, you should talk to Walter for a few minutes. A tough-love man, this Walter Gretzky.

I phoned Walter on the first Saturday morning in January. He almost torpedoed my trip.

"Don't have a rink this year. Too warm," he said of what had indeed been one of the warmest early winters on record.

I asked him when he thought it might get cold enough to make ice. "Ohhhhh, you know, the kids are getting older now . . . Brent's fourteen . . . I don't think I'll have a rink this year. Shame, eh?"

"A shame," I agreed. We exchanged small talk and said good-bye. Like many others, I'd thought of the Gretzky family rink as being less a slice of pastoral Canadiana and more a practical springboard created by an ambitious father as a means of launching his sons into the big-bucks world of professional hockey. But there was enough genuine regret in that "Shame, eh?" to make me think that Walter's rink — for whatever reasons it was first built — had worked its way so deeply into the fabric of the man's life that he would mourn its passing. Though in the end, he didn't let it die, as I learned in June of 1987 when I finally went to the Gretzky house as a guest at the Wayne Gretzky Tennis Classic. There in the yard were two regulation hockey goals resting on the grass about fifty feet apart in exactly the positions they must have occupied when the ice melted. The weather had eventually turned cold and . . . well, Walter can explain it. "Ohhhh, Brent, you know, he helped . . . and the kids around here wanted it . . . one more year, you know." But he built the rink the next year, too.

"I don't think he'll ever get rid of that thing," said Wayne. "I used to get him mad telling him I was going to put in a swimming pool." "There won't be any swimming pool," said Wayne in grumbling imitation of his father, including the expletive specifying precisely what kind of swimming pool there would not be. But in August of 1988 Walter accepted

Wayne's offer to install a pool. Coincidentally, and sadly, workmen broke ground for the pool on the same day Wayne was traded from the Edmonton Oilers to the Los Angeles Kings.

But the temporary absence of a Gretzky rink in January of 1987 left me facing the question of whether or not I wanted to drive about 2800 miles to skate on one family's vacant lot and in another's backyard.

"Fly," said Barb.

That I rejected the idea out of hand made me realize that, while I'd told Barb the truth about why I wanted to visit these people and skate on their rinks, I hadn't told her the whole truth. I wanted to take that long solitary drive for the same reason I often like to take long solitary skates. Driving, like skating, gives me a chance to be alone, my mind concentrated and wonderfully rid of anxiety, my body free to go wherever my blades or wheels can take me. I had a week in which I wanted to be totally free, and driving and skating were as close as I could come. Sipping cabernet sauvignon at 30,000 feet while strapped to a lounge chair is being comfortable. It is not being free. And it is certainly not being in control.

Crush the tee shot. That's the key to long-distance driving. Thus I'd planned to drive at least 700 miles on the first day. But snow squalls, the consequent late start, darkness and fatigue drove me into an Ashtabula, Ohio, motel after only 560 miles. I made some of that back the next day as I drove through the glass-and-steel towers of Cleveland, past the phallic silos of Indiana, those symbols of midwest fertility standing stark against the winter sky, north into the door-handle-to-door-handle traffic of Chicago and on up to snow-speckled and hilly Wisconsin. Barb was right. Tape selection was important. Collections of Mozart, Springsteen and the Beach Boys made up the bulk of my 18-tape traveling team. But as it got dark and I burned into my third tank of gas, I learned a truth of the American road: *There's no driving music like country music.* I'd gone to my bench — Waylon, Willie and Hank Jr. — long before I pulled into a hotel in Black River Falls, Wisconsin, short of my goal of Duluth, Minnesota, but leaving myself a mere 200-mile chip shot for the morning.

By two o'clock the next afternoon I was skating with Jerry Fryberger on the 90-by-40-foot rink beside his mother's home in Duluth. As we skated, Fryberger told me the history of the rink that is part of his father's legacy, his family's heritage and his community's inspiration. It is also — in its uncommon expanse — tangible evidence of the territorial imperative that seems to grip all rink owners. Indeed, at that moment I stood in unrepentant violation of every rink size limitation treaty I'd ever agreed to with Barbara. Weeks earlier I had extended the eastern border of my rink across the western border of the vegetable garden. But no backyard rink builder I'd ever known went as far as Jerry's late father, Bob Fryberger Sr.

Bob Fryberger was a 1929 hockey all-American at Dartmouth College and, later, a successful mining company executive. In 1943 he flooded a small section of his backyard so that his sons — Jerry and twin brother Bob Jr. and their younger brother Dates — would have a place to learn to skate. It was nice but too small. The next year Bob Sr. put a bigger rink on the side lawn. Still too small. So in 1947 he flooded the adjacent vacant house lot he owned to create a rink that would last for more than forty years. "When we were young we'd just tumble out the door and skate all day," says Jerry.

But even this wasn't enough for Bob Sr. While maintaining the rink on the vacant lot, the elder Fryberger bought land on nearby Lewis Street and persuaded friends and neighbors to build a full-size outdoor hockey rink and to form the Glen Avon Hockey Association (named after the local Glen Avon Presbyterian Church the Frybergers belonged to). In 1955 a Bob Fryberger-coached Glen Avon peewee team won the national championship in a tournament held in New York's Madison Square Garden. That team was made up mainly of boys who'd skated in the pickup games in the rink beside the Fryberger house and included future Olympian and Boston Bruins star Tommy Williams and 1964 Olympian Dates Fryberger. "You just can't take a bunch of kids from a four-block area and win a national championship. But that's what my father did," says Jerry, still justifiably amazed at what his family's rink hath wrought.

But even if Bob Sr.'s players had never won anything, the man would still stand as a virtual Copernicus of youth hockey, re-ordering as he did all conventional attitudes with his discovery that, in the universe of hockey, the game revolves not around the checkbook, but around the shovel. All Glen Avon teams had a policy requiring a parent from each family with a child in the program to be assigned to one of several eight-person ice cleaning and maintenance crews. "It was a practical necessity, but it also got everyone involved. We had great spirit among the parents," Jerry recalled. It remains a remarkable accomplishment in a sport where parents often have well-deserved reputations for cantankerousness. I've seen coaches verbally abused and physically threatened at youth hockey games and I once saw a parent reach over the glass of an indoor rink in an effort to hit a referee while a game was in progress. (Tell you what, guy. Let's shovel this eight-inch snowfall off of this 200-by-85-foot rink and then let's see how much energy we have for punching out the refs.)

Bob Fryberger Sr. died in 1957 when the car he was driving was hit head-on by a truck while northbound in a snowstorm on Route 61. Her grief notwithstanding, Mrs. Lavern Fryberger, Bob's widow, kept up the family's legacy.

"Mother's the one who kept this thing going," said Jerry as we walked from the rink to his mother's house. "It would've been easy for her to throw up her hands and say 'the heck with it' when Dad died."

It was worth the 2800-mile round trip just to meet Lavern Fryberger. Patrician-looking in a blue suit and ivory blouse, she served us tea and cookies at a kitchen table upon which sat catalogues from Tiffany's and Brooks Brothers. Lavern sat down to join us, but you would have needed a seat belt to keep her in her chair once we started talking about her rink. In less than five minutes she was on her feet demonstrating the proper way to walk across expensive Oriental rugs while wearing hockey skates. "You have to put the blade down flat, like this," she said, taking a succession of flat-footed steps that made her look rather like an ostrich. "If you put the heel or toe down first you'll cut the rug. On cold days I used to let the boys put their skates on in the house as long as they walked like this across the rugs," she said taking another ostrich step.

"I keep this rink for the smaller kids. It's a learn-to-skate rink," she said of the rink beside the house. She explained that the old Lewis Street rink gave way to a housing development, but that the city maintains both an indoor and an outdoor rink at nearby Comeau Field. She didn't tell me, but I later learned that the indoor rink is named after her late husband.

Lavern also policed the rink. "If I see any big hockey players pushing around the little kids on our rink, I'm out there like an old washerwoman," she said, again sitting down at the table. "I love to keep this rink going. It's activity. It's life."

With Bob Jr., Jerry and Dates all attending Middlebury College in Vermont, where they played on the same line in the 1960s, Lavern relied on friends, neighbors and skaters to keep the ice shoveled. She also developed a clever move for dealing with that most loathsome of outdoor rink skaters, the kid who will wait for the ice to be cleared before he shows up with his stick and skates. Jerry still laughs when he recalls a few of these bozos phoning Lavern to see if the ice was ready.

" 'You *betcha,* Billy'," says Jerry in high-pitched and enthusiastic imitation of his mother. " 'Come on over. You're going to have a wonderful time.' And of course the ice wouldn't have been shoveled at all and when the kid got here Mother would have a brand new shovel to hand him."

At the time I visited, Jerry — who lives a few blocks away with his wife Carol — was using a snowplow on a Jeep to clean the ice. He resurfaced two or three times a week by attaching a fire hose to a nearby hydrant. Like most rink owners I've met, Jerry regards snow removal as grunt work and ice making as art. He'll let you grab a shovel but the hose belongs to him, although that didn't stop one friend from trying.

It was late on a weekend night. A neighbor — dressed in jacket, tie, dress pants and an expensive overcoat — had just returned from a party where, Jerry said, "he might have had a few drinks." With his neighborliness fueled by alcohol, the man insisted on helping Jerry resurface the ice. "At first I refused, but he got so overbearing about it that I finally gave him the hose," said Jerry. Not content with laying down a gentle spray, the neighbor insisted that Jerry open the hydrant valve all the way. "I never turn on the water full force because I don't want it to eat holes in the ice, but this guy kept hollering, 'turn 'er up,'" said Jerry who, in this case, did open the valve all the way. The resultant surge of water ripped the hose out of his neighbor's hands and sent it thrashing about on the ice like some berserk brass-headed anaconda with the startled neighbor in slipping, squatting pursuit. "He got a grip on the hose, but below the nozzle, so it sprayed all over him. Then he fell on the ice and was twisting around in the water in his good clothes. I turned the water off. I'm just glad he didn't get hit by the nozzle," said Jerry sounding glad but not too glad.

Later that afternoon Jerry and I visited neighbors Bob and Phyllis Verchota, whose son Phil played on the 1980 U.S.

gold medal-winning Olympic hockey team and the 1984 team as well, and whose development as a player came about largely through the Glen Avon system and pickup games at the Frybergers' rink. Lest you think that the 1980 Miracle on Ice has been tossed into the broom closet of great sports memories, note that the evening before I met them, Bob and Phyllis viewed the videotape of the gold medal-clinching game for what must have been the umpteenth time, and here was Bob Verchota still steaming about a roughing penalty called on his son with four minutes and fifteen seconds remaining — "that wasn't roughing" — and there was Phyllis saying, "I almost couldn't watch."

We talked about the Frybergers' rink. "That rink was the hub of the neighborhood," said Phyllis, who credits it with much of her son's success. "In the life of every good hockey player you'll find an extra sheet of ice. For Phil it was the Frybergers' rink."

"We're rich because of it," said Bob, who celebrated the return on this wealth by firing his shotgun off the family's front porch on that Friday night in 1980 when the Yanks beat the Russians.

Maybe it's a peculiarity of Minnesota hockey mothers, but start talking about rinks and Phyllis Verchota — like Lavern Fryberger — gets her game face on in a hurry.

"Pancakes," she says contemptuously of today's youth hockey players, whom she apparently thinks wouldn't know a pickup game from a pickup truck. "Today's kids are pancakes. They don't know what it is to shovel the ice or to play in ten below. Remember the old ten-below rule, Jerry?"

Jerry remembers. "We'd cancel practice only if the temperature fell *below* ten below," said Jerry. "Hell, ten below is half of January . . . of course, we'd play on our backyard rink in any temperature."

Jerry echoed Phyllis's lament on the passing of pickup games such as he and his friends used to play on the family rink. "A few years ago I told a peewee team I was coaching, 'Kids, today we're going to play shinny.' One kid said, 'What's shinny, Mr. Fryberger?' I said shinny is where you don't know for a half hour who's on your team."

Phyllis laughed knowingly.

"Shinny's good for stickhandling," said Bob, who didn't talk much during my visit but who, in the end, spoke plainly and eloquently about the community spirit engendered by the Frybergers' rink. "Jerry, if you ever need any help, you just let me know," he said as he walked us to the door.

Driving back to his mother's house, I asked Jerry how much longer he'd keep the rink. "The only way there won't be a rink is if I move out of town and take my hose with me," he said.

• • •

It started snowing at 6:30 the next morning as I drove north out of Duluth headed for my last stop, artist Ronn Hartviksen's house in Thunder Bay, Ontario. It was a heavy, wet snow that made the road slippery. I thought about turning back and, in retrospect, I probably should have. On a dry, flat interstate my Mercury Colony Park wagon was a living room on wheels, but on snowy hills the front-heavy car was more like a luge sled with a roof rack. I white-knuckled it every time I saw a logging truck hammering toward me in the southbound lane.

I'd brought one album for this part of the trip and I shoved it into the tape deck. Bob Dylan (born Robert Allen Zimmerman) grew up in nearby Hibbing, Minnesota, and it seemed somehow appropriate to play his music while I was so close to his hometown. So I drove through places named Knife River and Castle Danger with the raspy voice of the poet of my generation pouring out of the speakers . . .

You never understood that it ain't no good
You can't let other people
Get your kicks for you.

The man at Canadian Customs was amusing if not encouraging.

"Destination?" he asked looking up at the snow.

"Thunder Bay," I said.

"You hope," he said.

It had stopped snowing by early afternoon when I reached Hartviksen's house on the outskirts of the city. I'd never met Ronn, but we'd corresponded for a couple of years after he'd read an article I'd written about my backyard rink. His notes, written on stationery adorned with his artwork — a water color of a Cree Indian camp, a pencil drawing of a sitting room — were filled with rhapsodic passages about even the most prosaic facets of rink maintenance:

- On shoveling: "It's the best medicine I've found for the mid-Arctic blues, a satisfying purchase of fresh oxygen inside of nature's Nordic theater." (I don't know, Ronn, I always thought it was mainly a pain in the back.)
- On finding pucks in the spring when the snow melts: "Outside the boards, the sun has exposed the rims and flat planes of errant pucks scattered like quotation marks re-echoing the zestful enthusiasm that once buried them there." (I picked up 83 such pucks one spring, Ronn, and my only thought had nothing to do with zestful enthusiasm. It had to do with telling those kids to keep their shots *down*.")

Several of Hartviksen's letters contained snapshots of art-work he'd painted on his ice. There was the Philadelphia Flyers logo with number 31 in the middle, a tribute to Philly goalie Pelle Lindbergh, who died in a 1985 car accident; a silhouette of a boy in a wheelchair, a silent cheer for Canadian cancer victim Rick Hansen's wheelchair trip around the world; and various Christmas and holiday greetings. In a letter to me Hartviksen described his ice painting as "the bunting and celebratory accents that add to the rink's character."

Frankly, I'd formed a picture of Hartviksen as being something of an odd character. But that didn't prepare me for his emerging from the house wearing a blue Japanese robe and brandishing a machete. "I carve the design in the ice with the machete, then paint it with a pigment wash. The robe — it's called a *hon-tong* and was a gift from a friend — keeps me warm and it has three-quarter sleeves, which leaves my arms free." He said he did most of his ice painting between two and five in the morning, when the severe cold ensures that the paint will freeze before it runs. I wondered what my neighbors would say if they were to see me on the rink at 3 A.M. dressed in a *hon-tong* and swinging a machete. Like Lucy Ricardo, I would have some 'splaining to do.

Hartviksen traded in the robe for a running suit and walked me out behind his house to see the 66-by-36-foot rink, the boards made of plywood and two-by-fours topped with chicken wire. About five inches of snow covered the ice. Without either of us saying anything, we grabbed shovels and went to work. As we shoveled, Hartviksen told me something former Canadian National Hockey Team head coach Dave King once said: "You can't love the game unless you've shoveled the ice." I should have it inscribed on my boards.

"Shovel along that goal line to the right of the net," Hartviksen said. I took a wide scraper and began pushing snow along the goal line toward the boards. Then I looked down and suddenly stopped. Hartviksen laughed. There, under my feet, in graceful two-foot script, was — my name. "Machete calligraphy," said Hartviksen.

As we shoveled and talked I began to get the feeling that Hartviksen's rink was appreciably different from the Frybergers', the Gretzkys' or mine. The other rinks existed principally for hockey and recreation. While Hartviksen's then-eleven-year-old son Galen and his friends played a lot of hockey on this rink it was clear that Ronn's interest went well beyond the game. This was a private place, a frame and canvas for personal expression and, as Ronn called it, "my frozen Walden . . . a lot of problems get solved when I'm working out here."

Later he showed me a book he calls his "Ice Log" in which he records temperatures, ice conditions and thoughts about the rink. An entry: "For over half the year work on our rink bridges events from the World Series to the NHL playoffs . . . it's a heartbeat carrying a seasonal pulse through our northern winters. [It is] no untouching ending when our lady of the ice merges back into the soil in a veil of tears and meltwater."

Galen came home from school and joined us for an impromptu hockey game. At first we just shot at the nets, but that soon evolved into three-man line rushes one way with the last skater into the offensive zone remaining back to play defense on the return two-on-one rush. No sides. No score. No time limits. Just the freewheeling joy of the game. We skated until we were sweating and tired. Galen went indoors to practice his saxophone while Ronn hauled out the garden hose to begin the resurfacing and I sucked on a beer his wife Margaret had dropped to me from the kitchen window. Ronn put his bare thumb over the hose nozzle to create the soft spray he wanted. "Isn't that cold?" I asked.

"No mosquitos, eh?" he said. Hartviksen seems to find connections most of us miss.

We ate dinner in a Japanese restaurant in the Port Arthur Curling Club at a table beneath a Hartviksen mural depicting the origins of curling. "I like giving eloquence to a surface like a wall or a sheet of ice," he said. There seems to be a streak of sidewalk artist in Hartviksen, who said he'd like to do a painting on a large municipal body of ice such as the pond in New York City's Central Park or Boston's Public Garden. But his all-time ice painting fantasy involved the now torn down but then very sad and solid Berlin Wall. "I wish there was a river running under the Berlin Wall. I'd like to paint a message on it. Something about freedom."

We said good-bye the next morning. As I threw my luggage into the car I noticed a small hand-lettered sign on the house. It was in a language I didn't recognize: *En Hav Perth Cov Gowan,* it read. "That's old Cornish," said Hartviksen. "It means 'In summer remember winter.'"

The trip home was filled with my antsy peekings at the clock and odometer. No fun. I played my tapes and tried to figure out what I'd learned from these people and their rinks. But most of the time I don't know what I think until I start to write it down.

I got home at 5:30 on a Friday evening, about three hours earlier than I'd told Barb to expect me. She'd planned a late dinner. In my absence a cold front had moved in and we had good ice on our rink. "Want to go skating?" Barb asked.

We put on our skates in the kitchen and Barbara asked me about the trip. I told her the first two things that popped into my head: about Hartviksen wanting to paint on ice near the Berlin Wall and about Mrs. Fryberger letting kids in skates walk on her Oriental rugs.

"Good values," said Barb, stepping out the kitchen door.

Coda — The Taj Mahal

The phone call came in early January 2000, almost twelve years to the week since I'd taken my drive through

Minnesota and Ontario to visit the Frybergers and Hartviksens. The call was from Danny Ronan, whom I'd known when he was a defenseman at Boston University, and he was calling from Ft. Wayne, Indiana, where he was playing with the Ft. Wayne Komets of the United Hockey League. He said there was this backyard rink in Woburn, Massachusetts, "that you absolutely have to see. . . . It's indoors. Artificial ice. Locker room. Unbelievable," he said, notwithstanding that Danny himself hadn't yet seen it but had only heard about it in phone conversations with his father, Ed, a neighbor of the rink's builder and owner, Bobby Holland.

I phoned the Holland household and got Bobby's wife Michele, who said I would be more than welcome to see the rink, which was "under an old greenhouse" and that "yes, we have a full compressor and ice-making system." She said this matter-of-factly like someone describing her backyard vegetable garden. She explained, "Bobby's Dad ran the Woburn town rink for nineteen years, so my husband knows how all the machinery works."

Barbara and I visited the Hollands late on a Sunday morning in February and were met at the door by Bob himself, who had been up since 5 A.M. to drive sons Bobby Jr., eleven, Alex, seven, and Danny, six, to early morning youth hockey games. The Hollands' daughter Michelle, thirteen, played a little youth hockey, then quit the game, but now, with the arrival of the new rink, was talking about playing in high school. Her father answered my first question before I asked it: "I didn't build this to make my kids pro hockey players," he said, gesturing out the kitchen window to where a one hundred-plus-foot semi-cylindrical greenhouse covered in white fabric dominated the backyard. "I'd be thrilled if they play high school hockey."

Bob Holland built his rink to shut down Nature's power play. "I'd had it with El Niño and La Niña and global warming and these winters where you only get two or three skating days. Too much work and not enough skating weekends. So we did this," he says, opening a side door that leads into what has to be the Taj Mahal of backyard rinks. Bob. Jr. is on the ice snapping shots into one of the rink's two full-size nets. The interior of the 100-by-30-foot rink is a compelling sight exceeding anything I'd ever seen in a lifetime in backyard sports. The ice contains a white paint and looks exactly like the ice in NHL arenas. Friends from the town rink help Holland etch in and paint the faceoff circles and dots along with the goal crease, blue lines, red line, goal lines and a big maroon "H" at center ice. The boards are painted white and have the same yellow plastic kick plate used in commercial rinks. "The kick plate helps me know how thick the ice is," Bob says. "I like to keep it one-and-a-half to two inches." He says it took twelve truckloads of fill to level his yard for the rink.

The ice looks perfect. Bob had just resurfaced it with what he calls his "Zamboni," a rig that looks like a triangle on a stick and is made of pipes. The "stick" screws onto a garden hose and water comes down the sides of the triangle and across the base, which is full of holes and has a cloth attached to the back. The water — Bob likes to resurface with hot water, "about a hundred and eighteen degrees," he says — flows out of the base plate and is spread evenly in about a two-foot swath by the cloth. "This is the best hundred and twenty-five dollars I ever spent," he said, hefting the Y-shaped rig with obvious pride.

Lights hang from the metal superstructure supporting the fabric of the greenhouse. Bob reaches up and bends back a small section of what looks like lightweight ceiling tile, revealing the aluminum foil beneath. "Insulation," he says. "Two layers." It is eighteen degrees inside the rink, about ten degrees colder than it is outside. "We can keep good ice until the outside temperature hits the low sixties," he says. "Then the ice gets a little soft. But we expect to be skating into late April."

Bob leads us through a wooden door into what looks like a combination snack bar and locker room. A long black bench runs along the back wall above which are metal clothes hooks and a shelf on which players can put gloves and other gear. On the opposite side of the room wooden stools stand empty behind a long counter in front of which two shatter-proof Plexiglas windows offer a view of the rink. The warming room has heat, wall-to-wall carpeting, a TV with VCR, a microwave and a fridge stocked with soft drinks. The stick rack is just inside the door, as it is in pro and college locker rooms. A hand-carved wooden sign on the wall reads "HOLLAND ARENA."

"We didn't start out this way," Bob says, looking out the Plexiglas window onto the rink. "We started with the boards and the plastic and with making all the beginner mistakes, just like everybody else." As Bob is talking the outside door opens and Ed Ronan walks in. Ronan's youngest sons, Greg, thirteen, and Matt, ten, are frequent skaters at the Holland Arena and Ed used to have a modest backyard rink of his own. "Did you tell them some of the stories?" Ronan asks Holland, who laughs and false starts a couple of times . . . "Ah . . . no . . . well . . . geez . . . ." Then, leading us back out into the yard, he points to a large transformer mounted on top of an electrical pole beside his house. "See that?" he says. "That's just for our house. We blew out the power in the neighborhood three times. The first time it was funny but after that there weren't many smiles." Of course, not everyone knew what hit them. "One day before Christmas the mailman told me he saw an elderly lady down the street taking down most of her Christmas lights," says Bob. "So he asks her what she's doing and she says, 'I blew out the power the other night. I must've put up too many lights this year.' The mailman said he didn't tell her what really happened. But we figured the best thing was to get our own power."

The only other problem was the steady loud hum coming from the compressor, the machine that pumps the refrigerant through the two-and-a-half miles of tubing under the ice. But a huge board leaning against the compressor housing serves as a sound baffle. Bob sticks his head into the compressor shed, glances quickly at two gauges and nods knowingly. "Twelve degrees going out and sixteen degrees coming in; that's about right," he says with the certainty of a man who spent much of his boyhood working in his father's commercial rink.

Bob takes us to his garage to show us his latest acquisition, a skate sharpening machine. "I have an electric score-board, too," he says. "It's a six-by-four thing my brother was throwing out of a rink he runs up in New Hampshire. But I haven't had time to rig it up yet."

"Does it have a penalty clock?" asks Barbara who, I feel compelled to point out to Bob, is the career penalty leader on our rink.

"We really haven't had any problems out here," he says. "The more kids on the ice the better. I like to see it busy. And we know all the kids who skate here. They're good kids." And it's a good thing they are because the Hollands could be seeing a lot more of them. Bob says he plans to leave the rink in place in the summer and replace the ice with solid flooring for roller hockey. "It took three months to put this up," he says, gesturing toward the greenhouse. "I don't want to go through that again every year."

We were about halfway through the forty-minute drive home when Barbara said, "You could skate a lot more if we had a rink like that."

"We'd all skate a lot more," I said.

It was about another minute before she said, "I think I'd skate less. I like to see the sky."

End Game

It began as a casual skate with my son Brian on the backyard rink on a Saturday morning when he was fourteen and I was forty-one. We'd gone out to pass the puck around for a half hour or so and were skating in easy figure eights just loosening up, and I don't think either of us knew how it started except that I remember he skated past me and I, trying to look casual, skated past him and he — maintaining the mutual charade of nonchalance — passed me, and the next thing we knew we were in a flat-out figure-eight race, leaning low and crosscutting vigorously behind the net, then sprinting diagonally across the ice before ducking low and skating hard through the next turn.

I was in front, but only because I was using my body to block Brian the way one stock car driver closes the gate on a faster car. I was taking up a lot of track and could hear Bri laughing as he tried to pass high on a turn only to have me squeeze toward the boards. The next time he tried to slingshot low on the turn but again I cut him off. It was obvious now that I couldn't outskate him the way I might have done the year before. On about the fourth or fifth lap, as we swung out from behind the net, I veered too wide, Brian cut inside and got his right shoulder in front of me, then easily outsprinted me across the ice and was pulling away as he swung into the next turn. I knew then — and I don't mean in retrospect; I mean at the very instant he went by me — that I'd never again be able to catch him. I comprehended the metaphor as clearly as I had the race. "Good-bye, Brian," I said to myself as he pulled away. I was happy for him. But if I had to point to a particular moment when middle age — the beginning of the inevitable and, I hope, long descent — officially began for me, it would be the final turn of that race, the instant Bri got that shoulder in front of me.

"Sooner or later every [player] comes to know that he is preparing himself for defeat, and perhaps humiliation," wrote Yale philosopher Paul Weiss in his book *Sport: A Philosophic Inquiry.* "His days are numbered, his successes rarely momentous, and his glories short-lived." Sounds like real life to me.

There was never much success or glory to begin with since I only played organized hockey at the school and CYO level and was a goalie on a team that recorded an undefeated season largely because they could score goals faster than I could let them in, which was very fast indeed. (I think we won a game 8-7 that season.)

But the final humiliation Weiss refers to didn't arrive until five years after Brian got that shoulder in front of me on the backyard rink. The telephone call was from my brother Patrick. "A bunch of us are renting the ice Sunday mornings at Saugus. We need one of those veteran stay-at-home defensemen. You want to play? C'mon. You still got some miles in the tank," is what the message on the answering machine said. But that is not what it meant. What I knew it meant was that my brother's group needed another body, and my ten bucks for ice rental was as good as anybody else's and that I should not even dream about playing any forward position or ranging more than five feet inside the offensive blue line.

I said I'd play. I should have known better.

It was a steamy Sunday morning in June when I pulled into the Saugus, Massachusetts, twin rinks parking lot. As soon as I opened the dressing room door I knew I was in trouble. The other players were in their twenties and thirties. I had just turned forty-six. One player was drinking beer. A couple of others looked like they would have been drinking beer if any was left. The "no checking, no slap shots" policy lasted about five minutes. I was more dangerously over my head than Captain Nemo in Jules Verne's *Twenty Thousand Leagues Under the Sea*.

On my second shift I went into the right defensive corner after a puck and was hit hard into the boards. I turned around to see who did it. It was Patrick. "Buy you a soda after the game," said Pat in a fair imitation of one of the Hanson brothers in the hockey movie *Slapshot*. That hit set the tone for the rest of the morning. Pat — who could probably recite the entire script of *Slapshot* from memory — would follow each check with a line from the movie. Whack! "And none of that stinkin' root beer . . ." His best line, and one not in the movie, came after he'd faked me outside, beaten me inside and scored. "My Linda Ronstadt move," said Pat. "Blew By You."

"How'd you do?" Barb asked when I got home.

"Disaster. I almost got killed," I said, slumping into a chair at the breakfast table. "Too old. No legs. No wind."

"You're catastrophizing," she said. Barbara is a social worker and she uses words like "catastrophizing." I laughed at the word but still felt depressed.

That week I ran three miles a day to try to get some stamina and leg strength and I dropped a few pounds largely by pulling old and about-to-be-replaced shingles off of my back porch roof, a job that, on broiling summer days, carries a coefficient of physical demand approximating that of harvesting sugar cane in Haiti.

I felt better when I went back the next Sunday. The feeling didn't last long. Opposing forwards cut around me as if I were a plastic cone in a skating drill. The highlight of my morning was the clanking of the rink doors swinging open to let the Zamboni roar out onto the ice like a snorting bull into the ring. We scattered like so many toreadors. It is hard-wired into a hockey player's psyche that Zamboni drivers and ice renters are natural enemies and that the drivers have the better of it in terms of armament.

I was among the first back to the dressing room, where I slumped onto a bench in the corner and tried to look inconspicuous. Patrick, who had played goal that day, came over and sat beside me.

"That was brutal," I said. "I should have to pay double."

"Hey, you blocked a couple of shots," he said.

"Guys who block shots have bad reflexes," I told him, stealing the line from ex-Philadelphia Flyer head coach Bob McCammon.

"At least you didn't do the old Flamingo," said Pat, suddenly standing on one leg and cringing as an imaginary shot whizzed by. "Ahhh, it wasn't like you were the worst one out there."

"I was the worst sober one out there," I said. Pat laughed.

"Hey, I hope I'm still playing when I'm your age," he said. He meant it kindly but it nicked me, a flesh wound to the ego.

I played the next Sunday because I didn't want to be a quitter. But then I realized there's a big difference between quitting and letting go. I knew it was time to let go.

The problem was that I took it too far. I didn't merely "let go" of trying to play hockey with younger and better players. But, the following spring, I gave up hockey, period.

It was around this time that I was writing a monthly column for the late and sporadically lamented *Inside Hockey* magazine. In what was, in retrospect, a self-indulgent and probably self-absorbed column, I told readers I was going to go a full calendar year without watching a school, college or pro game, without watching a telecast of a game and without setting foot in a rink with the single exception of my backyard rink. I planned to spend plenty of time skating but none passively watching.

"Middle age hockey crisis," said Barb when I showed her the column.

"At least I didn't buy a Corvette," I said.

Among my cockamamie rationalizations for a sabbatical from hockey were that "the unexamined game is not worth playing" and that I thought it would be "interesting to see what I had by not having it." And there is some truth in both of those statements. But, at murky bottom, I think there also lurked some sulky bitterness: If I couldn't play this game at any level, then, well, who needs it.

I almost made it. I hung tough for 47 weeks. Didn't watch a game in person or on television. I figured I reclaimed somewhere between 500 and 700 hours that otherwise would have been spent traveling to and from games and watching hockey live or on TV. But almost none of that "surplus" was spent on the backyard rink. I skated about as much as I'd skated in other years. Instead, I filled the time with books, and indeed began my self-imposed hockey abstinence by reading Shelby Foote's three-volume 3200-page *The Civil War: A Narrative,* a riveting account of how the South lost the war but beat the spread. But reading, while pleasurable and beneficial, can also be isolating, and it is a short step from isolation to disconnection, as I was about to discover.

I have always been inept at what commonly passes for casual social conversation, partly because I don't like what I see as the slithering insincerity of it but mostly because I can't think of much to say after "Hello." Barbara has a name for my behavior at, say, a brunch or cocktail party. "Bump-and-run socializing," she calls it. A quick "Hi, howareya. Catch you later," and I'm bouncing away, not entirely innocent of the insincerity penalty I'm too quick to call on others. My friends will not let me forget the time we were attending a birthday party and the hostess spotted me in an adjacent room, lying on the floor making Lego houses with her kids. "Why aren't you out here with the rest of us?" she asked. "Because I don't want to meet anyone I don't already know," I said, honestly but without thinking of how stupid it sounded.

But hockey was always different. I talk easily about the game, and hockey, for me, has been the entering wedge in many an enduring friendship. You can argue, with some justification, that hockey is a pedestrian and inconsequential subject. But, for me, it is the conversational access ramp to a highway that leads to more elevated topics and sustained relationships. My first date with Barbara was to a hockey game. My late father and I had the usual problems that so often divided the World War II generation from the Woodstock and Vietnam generation. But we never had a problem or spoke an angry word in a hockey rink.

• • •

My original intention was to give up hockey from May 1991 to May 1992. It was in April of '92 that I began thinking about not completing my year. It started on a night that Brian was watching an NHL playoff telecast. He suggested I watch it with him. "It'll make a better column if you don't last a year," he said.

But I didn't watch. I went to bed and read and, in doing so, passed up an opportunity to share something with one of my children. We are the sum of our decisions, and I'd chosen to be apart. I knew before I put down my book and turned out the light that I'd made a bad choice.

A few days later I deliberately stepped off the wagon, not by watching an NHL game but by watching a couple of nephews play on a local squirt team and watching a few playoff telecasts with Brian and whoever else was around.

I never got back to that 500 to 700 hours per year of watching or traveling to hockey games and I probably never will. I see a couple of college games, attend two or three Bruins games, watch a dozen or so NHL telecasts. It's enough to stay connected with people who matter to me.

In the end, all I learned from my forty-seven-week Ramadan is that George Bernard Shaw was right: "The worst and silliest of all wastes and sacrifices is the sacrifice of the power of enjoyment."

My resolution was well broken. In moving further from hockey I came no nearer to myself or anyone else. Hockey, for me, may not be the whole social archipelago, but it is an important island and, without access to it, other islands become harder or impossible to reach. Hockey connects. But only if you let it.

"Divorce is the affirmation of marriage," a college professor once told me, pointing to statistics showing that most people who get divorced eventually marry again. But what I think he meant is that remarriage is the affirmation of love.

A Skate with the Great One

It lives on only in memory, fading photographs and flickering home movies and has long since been replaced by a swimming pool; but the most consequential backyard rink ever built was the one Walter Gretzky constructed on a slightly concave stretch of lawn behind the family home at 42 Varardi Street in Brantford, Ontario. The "Wally Arena" is the rink that helped make Walter's eldest son Wayne the most incomprehensibly gifted goal scorer of all time.

"I built it in self-defense . . . so I wouldn't have to stand around freezing in all those town rinks watching Wayne practice," Walter said on November 22, 1999, the night Wayne was inducted into the Hockey Hall of Fame in Toronto. Well, maybe. But Walter also must have known that the best way to learn to play hockey is not only to be skating wind sprints and three-on-twos at the local rink but to supplement team practices with time alone: time spent skating, stickhandling and — through a mysterious osmosis that seems to occur in some but not others — internalizing the feel of puck, stick, blades and ice into an instinctive comprehension of the game, an assimilation surpassing our, or even his, understanding.

Wayne Gretzky threading his way through a slalom course of plastic laundry detergent bottles on his backyard rink in the 1960s is hockey's equivalent of Pele dribbling a tied up bundle of rags through the alleys of Tres Coracoes, Brazil, in the 1940s. What was ultimately happening on that backyard rink, and in those Brazilian alleys, was the acquisition of genius.

Indeed, the first time I heard the name Gretzky it was closely followed by the word genius. I was working, unhappily, at a Boston advertising agency in February 1974 when my father called from Quebec City, where he was coaching the Boston Junior Braves in the annual International Peewee Hockey Tournament, youth hockey's equivalent of the Little League World Series. "Would Boston University like to win about four NCAA championships?" he asked me. Boston U. is my alma mater.

"Who you got?" I asked, assuming my father had spotted some future star among the seventeen- and eighteen-year-olds in the Quebec area's superb junior A league.

"This kid's a peewee. His father says he might go to college if he doesn't turn pro. The boy could be the best thing since Orr," said my father, who did not drink and was not much inclined toward hyperbole. Comparing an eleven-year-old to Bobby Orr, the most complete hockey player of all time, was even harder to accept after my father explained that, no, the kid wasn't big or particularly strong or blazingly fast or possessed of an exceptionally hard shot.

"What's his game?" I asked.

"He's a genius at scoring goals," my father said. "How does three hundred goals sound? And something like a hundred assists. Kid wins his league scoring title by something like two hundred points." (The actual figures were 378 goals, 120 assists, and 498 points in 69 games,)

I asked who the kid was.

"Wayne Gretzky," my father said. "Remember the name."

I didn't have to remember it because, starting shortly after my father's call, the American media discovered the kid Canadians were already calling "The Great Gretzky," and the name became a staple of U.S. sports reportage for more than two decades. Which is why, in January of 1984, having happily traded the advertising business for magazine journalism, I found myself on a flight from Boston to Edmonton to write a *Sports Illustrated* cover story on Gretzky, who was torching the NHL record book. The news hook on my story was a period in which Gretzky had scored a point or more in forty-one consecutive games, a feat many were comparing to Joe DiMaggio's fifty-six-game hitting streak in 1941. Gretzky would run that streak to forty-six in the four games I was with him and would eventually extend it to fifty-three games, a record that may stand forever.

But the highlight of that trip for me wasn't the streak; it was the chance to talk to Walter, the King of the Backyard Rink Builders.

I did one of my interviews with Wayne on a flight from Edmonton to Detroit. We hadn't talked for ten minutes before the conversation turned to the Wally Arena. Wayne said his normal routine while growing up was to skate by himself in the morning before school and again with his friends after school from about 3:30 until his mother Phyllis called him to supper which, for Wayne, was little more than a change on the fly. He'd often sit at the table while still wearing his skates and rush back to the rink — either alone or with Walter — as soon as he finished eating.

Weekends were nothing but a hockey marathon. Skate till you drop. "There'd be skates and equipment all over the house and yard on a Saturday. Drove Wally crazy," said Wayne, obviously enjoying the nostalgic look back more than the ensuing and disconcerting look forward. "I know I'm never going to be able to live like that," he said, reflecting on what he knew would be the want of privacy because of his fame as his country's most recognizable celebrity. "Too bad."

I met Walter in Detroit, where Wayne picked up two more goals and an assist to run his streak to forty-three games. Walter and a group of friends had driven to Detroit from Brantford and would drive back after the game so that Walter could be on his job as a Bell Canada repairman first thing next morning. At first I found Walter reticent and guarded, apparently not overly trusting of writers. Because this contrived "interview" was going nowhere and because I didn't want to stand in the way of letting a father watch his son play, I put away my list of prepared questions and let the conversation go wherever Walter wanted to take it. Responding to the collective murmur that swept through the Joe Louis Arena crowd of 19,557 every time Wayne touched the puck, Walter asked, "How'd you like to live like that? People expecting a miracle every time you step on the ice. That's pressure." Later, when Wayne beat Detroit goalie Greg Stefan — Wayne's boyhood friend and former peewee teammate — Walter neither stood nor cheered. "Poor Greg," said Walter, "I drove to the game with his father. Wayne never had a bigger fan than Frank Stefan."

But with Wayne off the ice I played the card I'd had, almost literally, up my sleeve. I showed Walter a couple of Polaroid photos my father had given me, of a shaggy-haired, scrawny eleven-year-old in an oversized Brantford hockey jacket tobogganing with a group of his teammates and the Boston Jr. Braves players in Quebec City in 1974. "I think you met my father," I said. Walter laughed, said he remembered my father and the Jr. Braves, and immediately the conversational gates swung open. It wasn't long before we were talking less about Wayne and more about our families and backyard rinks.

Walter explained that he made his rink by tamping down a layer of snow and letting a lawn sprinkler run all night. I said that, because it was warmer in southern New England than in Ontario, I had to use a plastic liner and a corral of boards. And we both commiserated about our kids coming in at night and leaving equipment strewn all over the ice.

Walter said he never pressured Wayne to practice (a fact Wayne corroborates), "But you just couldn't keep him off the ice."

Even with his eldest son in the NHL, Walter told me he kept the backyard rink going for Wayne's younger brothers, Keith, Glen and Brent, and for other kids in the neighborhood: "Still out there with the sprinkler every night."

The Wally Arena is the reason there was always a little rink rat in Gretzky's game, and after the win in Detroit I asked Wayne about the most valuable lessons he'd learned from his father on the backyard rink. "One hundred percent of the shots you don't take don't go in," he said, laughing. He also said it was Walter who told him to always go into the boards while turning; never go straight in "where some-one can line you up for a hit and get all of you. If you're turning they'll only get a piece of you."

"Timing," said Walter when asked what he thought was the biggest benefit of the hours spent on the backyard rink. "He has the timing to strip a guy of the puck. He's on them before they know it."

That timing was dramatically showcased two nights later when the Oilers played in Chicago and Gretzky was point-less with less than ten seconds to play. With the score 4-3 Edmonton, the Blackhawks had pulled goalie Tony Esposito in favor of an extra attacker and were pressing the Oilers in Edmonton's defensive zone. Gretzky was in the high slot, sneaking glances at the clock and waiting for a chance. With seven seconds to play, the puck finally left the Oilers' zone, where it was retrieved in neutral ice by Chicago forward Troy Murray, who tried to flip the puck forward to teammate Doug Wilson. But Gretzky — in a series of moves right out of a backyard game of keepaway — flicked the pass out of mid-air with his stick, batted it to the ice with his glove, used his body to shield off the backchecking and aghast Murray, skated into the Chicago zone and slid the puck into the empty Blackhawks net to secure the win, beat the clock and extend his streak to forty-four games. "GRET-sky sucks! GRET-sky sucks!" chanted the huge Chicago Stadium crowd while, on the ice, a smiling Gretzky was mobbed by his teammates.

The streak hit forty-five in Buffalo when Gretzky assisted on his team's lone goal in a 3-1 Edmonton loss and it jumped to forty-six in New Jersey when Gretzky picked up three assists in a 5-4 Oiler win after which he admitted, "The pressure to get a point every night is beginning to bother me a little."

As Gretzky pushed his streak toward fifty-three I sat down to write a story I hoped would convey not only the consummate excellence of Gretzky the Hockey Player — that had been well chronicled at this point — but would also give readers a feeling for what I found so compelling about Gretzky: that besides his skill he seemed to be sustained by an almost childlike joy in the game, buoyed by a pure love of skating and of hockey. While in Gretzky's Edmonton penthouse I'd noticed a portrait of Wayne painted by the late pop artist Andy Warhol. It was one of six paintings Warhol had done of Gretzky. Gretzky told me five of the paintings would be sold to raise money for charity but that he wanted to keep one. He displayed it opposite a print of Warhol's famed portrait of Marilyn Monroe. On a whim — and to get some different third-party perspective on my subject — I phoned Warhol to ask what he saw when he looked at Wayne Gretzky through the eyes of an artist. And with an artist's concision, Warhol said, "What I see in Wayne is great joy and energy."

It's what I saw, too: an admixture of spunky happy rink rat supporting Gretzky's otherwise polished and sophisticated game.

What I didn't know when I filed that story is how much closer to that "joy and energy" I was about to get and what a view I would have.

• • •

In late January of 1985, about one year after I'd written the Gretzky "streak" story, I found myself, per order of my editors, on another flight to Edmonton in pursuit of yet another cover story on Gretzky, who had by then led the Oilers to their first Stanley Cup, won his fifth league MVP Trophy and, on January 13, 1985, scored his 400th NHL goal to reach that level seventy games earlier than Mike Bossy, who previously had been the fastest player to 400. Gretzky had also become — at age twenty-three — only the eighteenth player to reach 1000 points, accomplishing in five-and-a-half seasons what took the other seventeen an average of sixteen seasons. Gretzky was simply too hot to ignore.

Facing two weeks on the road, most of it in Edmonton, Alberta (which my daughter Tracey once described as "the second province from the left"), I did something I'd never done before. I packed my skates. I knew that the photographer on the story — freelancer Paul Bereswill — had occasionally skated with members of the maintenance crew at what was then called Northlands Coliseum, and I thought I might be able to join in and kill a little downtime.

The story went badly almost from my arrival. I went to the games, went to the practices and interviewed Gretzky's teammates, friends, opponents, coaches, agents and anyone remotely connected with my story. But all I got was what I call "refried beans" — essentially the same quotes I'd heard the year before only in new words. After a week of reportorial mucking and grinding I still lacked a clear new angle on Gretzky and any colorful or truly insightful third-party perspective. It was on the team's one road game during that stretch — an overnighter in Vancouver, British Columbia (first province on the left) — that I ran into then-Edmonton head coach Glen Sather in the lobby of the Westin Bayshore Hotel following the Oilers' 4-4 tie with the Canucks, in which Gretzky had bunted in a goal when a puck popped out of the glove of Vancouver goalie Richard Brodeur.

"How you coming on your story?" Sather asked, more to make small talk than out of genuine interest, I thought.

"Not too well," I said.

"Aren't the guys cooperating?" he asked.

"Gretz and the players have been great," I said. "The problem is that I can't find a new angle."

"Well, let us know if there's anything we can do to help," said Sather, dismissively I thought. I didn't expect that level of interest from an NHL head coach (there are high school coaches who wouldn't have said that — which may in part explain why they're high school coaches) and I could hardly believe what I heard myself saying next.

"Would you let me skate with him?" I asked, voicing a thought that, frankly, did not just pop into my head in a blinding flash of intuitive brilliance as I strolled through the hotel lobby, but was an idea I'd been toying with for a few days — an idea born mainly of a writer's desperation. I was at the time a forty-year-old ex-goalie who had never played above the scholastic level. I had no illusions of keeping up with Wayne Gretzky. Instead, my idea was to skate with Gretzky for a few minutes on a pond somewhere. No photos, no publicity, just a brief skate on natural ice whereon I hoped to see Gretzky's boyish joy made manifest. I figured Gretzky still had enough rink rat in him to go for the idea. Indeed, Gretzky had told me that earlier that winter he'd gotten involved in a pickup game of road hockey with a bunch of friends, this in the heart of Edmonton. He said he pulled a stocking hat low on his head so he wouldn't be recognized.

Sather killed the pond-in-the-woods idea (no surprise there) but to my astonishment said, "We'll let you skate with him at practice."

All I could think of to say was, "Thanks. You say when. I won't be in your way long. I just want to see him from a new angle."

The one thing I *did not* want this session to be was a kind of journalistic fantasy camp. I had no realistic thought of trying to tell my readers, "This is what it's like to skate with Wayne Gretzky," because the inevitably embarrassing fact would be that I wouldn't be skating *with* Gretzky but well *behind* him. All I wanted to do was position my journalistic lens in a new place so that readers might see Gretzky from, literally, a new angle.

We returned to Edmonton where, on a Saturday, the Oilers won the second game of the home-and-home series with Vancouver 7-5 with Gretzky scoring from behind the net by banking a shot off Brodeur's skate. The next day was Super Bowl Sunday and Sather cancelled practice. But with ice time available at Northlands I thought I'd get in an hour or so of skating just to get used to the rink and maybe cut down on the embarrassment factor. But when I got to the Coliseum, Oiler defenseman Paul Coffey — a sure-bet future Hall-of-Famer and one of the fastest and most technically perfect skaters since Bobby Orr — was on the ice with about a dozen youngsters, winners of a win-a-clinic-with-Paul-Coffey contest. Coffey and the kids were using only half the ice, so I skated down to the other end whereupon occurred the same phenomenon I've seen dozens of times on skating ponds: a kind of unplanned but inevitable blending where groups and individuals come together spontaneously—not by invitation of the group or intrusion by the individual but by a kind of insinuation of each to the other. You chase down a stray puck on a pond, pass it back to a player in the game and the next thing you know he's passed it to you and the most anyone might say is, "He's on our team."

After I'd chased down a few pucks coming out of Coffey's end of the ice, I found myself standing in the corner of the rink feeding soft passes to oncoming skaters in a skate-cut-and-shoot drill. As the kids took their shots and skated to the opposite corner of the rink, Coffey had something to say to each one. But he didn't bellow his advice as so many coaches do. ("HEY, NUMBER EIGHT. YEAH, YOU. LOOK BEFORE YOU SHOOT.") Instead he leaned over and almost whispered to each kid. I have no idea what he said, but I remember thinking that this wasn't the same guy who then had the reputation among writers of being cold, remote and a tough interview. Kids and open ice brought out the best in Coffey. And they brought out the rink rat in everyone.

The drills and coaching may have lasted forty minutes or so before structure gave way to the sheer joy of playing. For the final ten or fifteen minutes — and without anyone saying anything — the drills abruptly gave way to a game of keepaway with Coffey and me trying (OK, I was trying, Coffey was half-trying) to keep the puck away from a dozen laughing kids who chased after it like a swarm of bees. Even at what I fancied was half speed (I'd learn the next day it was more like one-quarter speed) Coffey had the best skating stride I'd seen since Orr's. The power flowed from his hips and drove his legs to full extension. There was no motion wasted. Nothing choppy or forced. As for me, overweight and out of shape (had I ever been *in* shape?), I almost collapsed on the players' bench in a combination of laughter and fatigue. A few parents were hanging around and all I remember saying to them was, "God, that was fun." So leveling and democratic is the freemasonry of hockey players that my thoughts were mainly on the kids until I said good-bye to Coffey and left the rink thinking, *I just skated with the best rushing defenseman since Orr and, while it was happening, it didn't feel any different from skating with a bunch of guys at Little Jennings Pond in my hometown or just fooling around with friends on the backyard rink.*

Skating at a team practice was to feel disquietingly different.

• • •

Because most NHL teams don't play on Super Sunday, the Oilers had a rare Monday night game, which meant they had what is known as a "morning skate" — a light half-hour non-contact workout that has more to do with psychological focus than with physical preparation. As a reporter, I routinely went to game-day skates in search of quotes, anecdotes or news. I didn't think Sather would let me skate with his team on game day, but I took my skates and a running suit just in case. I didn't even have to ask. Sather was walking out of the team room toward the practice ice when he saw me standing with a cluster of writers and broadcasters. "If you're skating with us, let's go," he said. He didn't have to say it twice.

• • •

The ice at Northlands Coliseum is still smooth with the morning resurfacing when I step through the door by the players' bench and self-consciously jump into the flow of players, all wearing their white, blue and orange game uniforms and all skating counterclockwise like some giant pinwheel. The first thing I notice isn't the sight of the players but the sound. Center Mark Messier and speedy winger Glenn Anderson fly by me, their skates ripping the ice ... SCRUNCH ... SCRUNCH ... SCRUNCH ... under the pressure of their tremendous leg drive. But a few seconds later Gretzky skates past me almost bouncing on his skates and the sound of the blades is a barely audible *swick ... swick ... swick ....* He's not going as fast as Messier, Anderson or Coffey, but there is more of a jump in his stride—a kind of weightlessness: he weaves among his teammates and seems somehow less anchored to the surface; a shorebird flitting happily among the troglodytes; a boy slaloming through the detergent bottles.

"Our first mistake is the belief that the circumstance gives the joy which we give to the circumstance," wrote Emerson. There are many players in the same circumstances this morning, going through the same practice, but Gretzky seems to have brought the biggest appetite, the happiest attitude, the most obvious love for the sheer joy of playing. It would be different later in New York in the nineties when Gretzky, then a Ranger, rarely practiced and, when he did, seemed more like a guy with a lunch box and a day's growth of beard trudging to the factory to put in his time. But this was the mid-eighties and the Great One was at his greatest.

To watch Gretzky is a pleasure, but to skate with him is a revelation and a privilege for a guy like me who, back then, still played pickup hockey on the ponds and on my rink.

Sather divides the team into three lines for a skate-and-shoot drill. Because I shoot left I jump into the line with the left wingers and Sather juggles people around so I end up skating with Gretzky at center and Finnish-born Jari Kurri on right wing. A pass from Gretzky to me is perfect — soft and on the black tape of my stick blade — and my only thought is to get the puck back to him before he's out of range. But my return pass is terrible, in his skates on his backhand side. In virtually one motion he flicks the puck off the blade of his right skate and onto his stick and snaps a shot between goalie Grant Fuhr's legs. On the rush back, Kurri leaves a pass for me in the slot but it seems somehow presumptuous or unprofessional to shoot — something a fantasy camper, not a journalist, would do — so I pass quickly to Gretzky, who immediately — and surprisingly — passes it back to me. But I'm determined not to shoot, so I again pass the puck back to him at the edge of the crease — he *has* to shoot now — and I begin gliding around the net. Incredibly, Gretzky centers the puck from behind the goal line, past goalie Andy Moog, and across the front of the crease to me. I have almost no choice but to tap it in. Gretzky raises his stick, smiles and yells as the puck clanks against the back of the cage.

We take one more rush, the final one in the drill. This time Kurri sits out and Gretzky and I trade passes as we move up ice, Gretzky holding himself back and weaving in a slalom-like course so as not to get too far ahead of me. Every time I give him the puck he gives it back and, as we draw closer to the net, it's apparent that he again wants to put me in a position where I have to shoot. But, embarrassed and feeling more than a little intrusive, I have made up my mind not to shoot no matter what. As Gretzky strides over the goal line I make a final pass to him and — the rush obviously over — I again begin swinging wide around the goal. But instead of merely gathering in the puck and lining up for the next drill, Gretzky, to the left of the goal and with his body already beyond the goal line, hits the brakes, whirls, reaches back over the goal line with the puck and clanks a backhander off of the far post and into the goal.

Gretzky yells, raises his stick, and deliberately spins and crashes into the glass behind the cage. Coming around the net I get a good look at his face. He is smiling, truly beaming. Warhol was right. There is joy and there is energy. The look on Gretzky's face is the same look I've seen on the faces of children on backyard rinks.

I raise my stick, too.

Roots in the Garden

A reporter for *The National Post* in Canada phoned recently to ask me about my backyard rink for a feature he was writing on the outdoor rink as an endangered species. When he asked how I came to build a rink in the first place, I launched into what is starting to feel like a stump speech. I told him that I built the rink to descend the ladder of sports evolution . . . to skate whenever I wanted to . . . for my kids and their friends to enjoy . . . for the advantage of being able to maintain good ice in my yard in a way I could never maintain it on a lake or pond, and so on.

My answers were true enough as far as they went, but neither the reporter's question nor my reply were sufficiently deep or revealing; they addressed the reasons for the rink but not its origins, its roots.

The better question would have been the one musicians, writers and artists constantly ask each other: *Who were your influences? Who, or what, makes you what you are?*

Had the reporter asked me this — or had I thought of it during the interview instead of afterward — I would have told him that my rink is of both common and noble parentage.

On the common and somewhat trashy side, one of my rink's progenitors was a cheap and laughably small "kit rink" I got for Christmas in the early 1950s. This almost completely useless contraption consisted of a long strip of aluminum roughly six inches wide, a small plastic liner such as one would find in a child's wading pool and a few clips to fasten the plastic to the aluminum. The whole thing was contained in a cardboard box with a drawing of a figure skater wearing a red skating dress trimmed with white fur and spinning rapturously on this little circle of ice as though she were on the main Olympic figure skating venue at Grenoble or Lake Placid. In reality, the aluminum formed a circle roughly eight to ten feet in diameter, and any figure skater performing on this small a surface for more than five minutes would have chopped the whole thing into a huge Slurppy. But this apparently didn't matter to my father, who, finding a flat place in the yard, assembled and flooded the rink. In a few days we had what can best and most charitably be described less as a rink and more as our own frozen puddle.

It was a Sunday morning after church when my father announced we were going to try out the new rink. He and my sister and I trooped into the cellar, she and I to pull on skates we'd received for Christmas and he to slip into a pre-World War II pair of skates with leather laces that kept breaking and which he'd repair by tying the lace back together with a square knot, apparently oblivious to the fact that while this provided a temporary solution to the problem it would later make the skate impossible to take off.

With our skates on, I grabbed a small goalie stick I'd been given for Christmas and he grabbed a regular hockey stick with a cracked and heavily taped blade and we walked across the cement floor of the cellar, grinding the bejesus off of whatever edges may have been on those blades (in my father's case the grinding may have improved his skates by knocking off the accumulated rust of a decade). My father said he was a goalie on a club team "before the War" (like many men of his generation, life was divided into three parts, "Before the War . . . during the War . . . after the War"), and I recall as a child seeing one or two photographs to support that claim. But what my father didn't know about skating and skate maintenance was well worth knowing.

As I pushed open the cellar door and we exited into the yard, still walking on our skates, my father began a brutally off-key and lyricless rendition of a march I'd never heard before: *Da-dum. Da-da-da-dum-dum. Da-dum. . . .* It wasn't pretty. My father couldn't have carried a tune in a goalie bag. "That's *'Paree',*" he explained. "It's the Bruins song." I had never seen the Bruins play, but since my father's first butchering of that song as we walked the eighty or so feet to our "rink" I have heard *"Paree!,"* as it's called in English, or *"Ça c'est Paris!,"* as it was entitled in the original French, more than a thousand times. It is still the Boston Bruins theme song — played when the team comes out for warmups, games and periods — and to this day it remains part of the soundtrack of my life, often playing in my mind when I walk down the plywood runway from my porch, step over the boards and take the season's first skate and at other random times throughout the year, most often when I'm skating alone. But on this Sunday in the fifties my father's rendition of the song was just another bizarre occurrence on a decidedly bizarre day.

It didn't take long for us to discover that our so-called rink was inadequate for hockey or recreational skating or just about anything. My father used his stick to skim pucks at me from a distance of maybe seven feet. If I missed the puck — something I did frequently — it would hit the aluminum siding and, as often as not, flip out of the rink into the snow. If I made the save — or, more accurately, if the puck hit me — the rebound would almost certainly fly out of the rink and land even deeper in the snow. What my sister was doing while all this puck shooting and retrieving was going on I don't know. Probably shuffling around the edges of the rink. Girls didn't play hockey in those days.

We were back in the cellar in less than a half hour and my father was already making plans to flood the backyard to create a bigger and better rink, though a year or two later, I would be the one trying, and failing, to flood the yard.

I don't think we ever again skated on that little aluminum circle, and yet its design — a retaining wall with a plastic liner — remains the basic one I've used for my own rink for the past seventeen years.

As we clomped back across the snowy frozen ground and down the three blade-destroying cement steps into the cellar, my father was humming *"Paree"* again. I can hear it as though it were yesterday, and it unfailingly transports me back to the days when I first met the building that was to be my backyard rink's royal parent and enduring inspiration. No building, no manmade structure of any kind, has ever appealed to my imagination, claimed my heart and consistently enhanced my life as did the recently demolished Boston Garden. My own rink — or perhaps more accurately, my desire to build and own a rink of my own — can be traced back to the Garden and, even beyond that, to the Hippodrome of P. T. Barnum.

• • •

It happened late on Sunday afternoons in the 1950s and early '60s. After the black and white images of Frank Gifford and Kyle Rote had faded from our television set, after broadcaster Chris Schenkel had made his last "overeager Giant" excuse for a Sam Huff late hit, after darkness had fallen, my father would turn in his armchair and begin the catechism: "You done your homework?" he'd ask. My answer — true or not — was always "Yes," or "I have a first-period study hall." Either reply elicited my father's invitation: "Bruins are home. You want to go to the Garden?"

Did I want to go to the Garden? Did I want to go to heaven when I died?

Affection for the Boston Garden began early when, as a five-year-old, I took a trip to see a gorilla. The Ringling Brothers Barnum & Bailey Circus posters portrayed Gargantua as a second King Kong, but viewed in his cage in the Garden's east lobby he was a large, ugly, rather docile anthropoid ape. The gorilla was a letdown. The Garden wasn't.

Glimpsed first from a ground level door not far from Gargantua's cage, the main arena stood flanked by three tiers of seats rising from a sawdust floor into a mysterious smokey-silver darkness pierced by spotlight beams, their cones transected by what looked to me like a million miles of rope. Spellbinding is not too strong a word.

I got a different look at the place several years later when my father took me to my first hockey game, a mid-season contest between the Boston Bruins and Detroit Red Wings. It was a night memorable mainly because of the goaltending of Detroit's Terry Sawchuck and Boston's Sugar Jim Henry, the battering physical play of Terrible Ted Lindsay (Lindsay was far more frightening than Gargantua) and, most of all, the Garden herself. Ice had replaced sawdust and, though the spotlights were gone, the arena remained a compelling sight, an eye-filling, wraparound, triple-decker spectators' tenement where you didn't merely watch a game but leaned over the railing and took part. It was, and for the more romantic always remained, what the late Eddie Powers, former Garden president, called "The House of Magic." But as I learned later when my growing obsession with the Garden led me to look up its history, it was hockey, not magic, that kept the old Garden going.

It wasn't planned that way. Circus impresario P. T. Barnum started it all in New York City in 1874 when he bought an old trolley car barn in Madison Square, renovated it to accommodate his circus, then hyperbolically renamed it the Great Roman Hippodrome. The word "Garden" — a popular euphemism for theater, a term which in those days reeked of dance halls and demon rum — first came into play a year later when bandleader Patrick Gilmore bought the place from Barnum and renamed it Gilmore's Garden.

Gilmore sold out in 1879 to a syndicate that renamed the place after its location: Madison Square Garden. But the Garden remained more of a rich man's toy than a good investment. Syndicates headed by W. H. Vanderbilt and, later, J. P. Morgan, owned the Garden and suffered substantial losses, though that didn't stop the Morgan group from building a new Madison Square Garden on the same site in 1887. Enter gambler-promoter George "Tex" Rickard.

While the Garden owners took a bath, it was another story for promoters. Rickard, a former saloon owner, borrowed $10,000 in 1916 to promote a prize fight at Madison Square Garden. He grossed $152,000 that night and made $5 million more on fights over the next five years. By 1924, when mortgage holder New York Life foreclosed on the Garden, Rickard was ready to make his move. He wanted the Garden to be the General Motors of sports arenas.

He would begin, he said, by building a new Madison Square Garden at 49th Street and Eighth Avenue, precisely twenty-three blocks from Madison Square (what could you expect from a man named Tex who was really from Kansas?). But Rickard didn't stop there. Flushed with success, not to mention money, he envisioned a national chain of sports arenas, all under the ownership of his Wall Street syndicate, Madison Square Garden Corporation. Boston — more accurately Boston Madison Square Garden — would be the second link.

It should be noted that Rickard believed in hockey almost as much as he did in boxing. He opened his New York building on December 15, 1925, with a hockey game between the New York Americans and the Montreal Canadiens. He later talked his friend Lester Patrick into putting a second hockey team in the Garden, a team Rickard named after himself — Tex's Rangers.

Less than three years after the New York opening, Boston Garden was ready for action, which is precisely what it got. The building opened with a fight followed by a hockey game (a sequence quickly reversed by later editions of the Bruins). On November 17, 1928, a full house got its Irish up watching Honey Boy Finnegan pound Andre Routis in a championship featherweight match. But if the opening night fight fans were enthusiastic, the first hockey crowd, three nights later, was out of control. The *Boston Herald* reported the night as ". . . a mob scene reenactment of the assault on the Bastille." About 17,500 fans — 3,500 more than either fire laws or seating plan permitted — jammed in to see the Eddie Shore-led Bruins face the Canadiens.

The only thing higher than attendance was emotion, as referee George Mallinson found out when he whistled a Bruins rush offside and someone in the stands threw a garbage can at him, more or less setting the tone for Bruins games yet to come.

In keeping with the frustrating (if only for Boston) Bruins-Canadiens tradition, Montreal's Sylvio Mantha beat Boston goalie Cecil "Tiny" Thompson with less than a minute to play in the second period for a 1-0 Montreal win. But the Garden was open and rolling. A 1928 Harvard-Yale hockey game drew a standing-room crowd of 15,000 and the Garden drew good crowds for high school hockey when it booked the Greater Boston Interscholastic League for Saturday afternoons. Rickard looked like a genius. But not for long.

In 1929 the Great Depression was born and Tex Rickard died. Boston Garden almost died, too. With crowds and gate receipts falling in New York and positively plummeting in Boston, the New York backers wanted out. They sold their Boston stock to the Boston Arena Corporation, a group that ran a smaller, older arena on the other side of town. The new owners pulled out every promotional stop — some prescient, some bizarre.

Take, for openers, the seven inches of dirt trucked in and packed on the Garden floor to accommodate a December 11, 1935, college football game between Notre Dame and a team of college all-stars. The field was eighty yards long "and a little narrow," Eddie Powers recalled. Punts bounced off the lights. Shades of the Arena Football League, still more than fifty years in the future.

Zanier by far was the great ski jump. In 1935, '36 and '37 the Garden installed a ski jump running from the balcony to the main floor. Original plans, mercifully abandoned, called for cutting a hole in the roof so the jump could start higher. The run was packed with crushed ice and landings were broken by bales of hay (if the skiers were lucky).

The new owners schemed and scratched for every dime, but in the end, the ice that made the Garden saved it. A Norwegian Olympian named Sonja Henie did a few waltz jumps between periods of a Boston Olympic vs. Jr. Canadiens hockey game and fans went wild. Thus was born the touring Sonja Henie Ice Revue, the Ice Follies (1937) and the Ice Capades (1940).

Eddie Shore wasn't much for waltz jumps, but by the late 1930s he was bringing crowds back to the Garden. Fans filled the building to its 13,909 hockey capacity to see Shore, goalie Frankie "Mr. Zero" Brimsek and the "Kraut Line" made up of Milt Schmidt, Woody Dumart and Bobby Bauer, three boyhood friends from the largely German neighborhoods of Kitchener, Ontario. Shore and company led the Bruins to the Stanley Cup in 1939, and even after Shore's 1940 retirement, the B's won the Cup again in 1941, and in the process saved the Boston Garden. They also saved part of my father's adolescence.

The Depression hit my father's family hard enough, he told me, that he had to put cardboard in his shoes to cover the holes in the soles. But he always seemed able to scratch up the twenty-five or fifty cents for a second balcony seat at a Bruins game. He said he could get so carried away by the excitement of a hockey game that he would sometimes become physically ill. Yet he began to fall away from hockey when he enlisted in the Army in February 1942. I can't recall his ever going to a hockey game when I was a child. He didn't start going until after my mother was hospitalized with what would prove to be terminal cancer in the winter of 1954. Then hockey seemed to re-emerge as a kind of emotional shock absorber, a role it would play for the rest of his life. It started when I came home from school for lunch one Thursday and my father said he had two tickets for that night's Bruins game. "You may as well know what you're watching," he said, grabbing a pad of lined paper and with a pencil drawing diagrams of icing and offside infractions. On that day and for the next fourteen years — until my marriage in 1968 — we would see hundreds of Bruins games together. He bought season tickets in 1962 (Section G, Row E, Seats 3 and 4) and when mid-sixties business reversals made holding onto those tickets a financial burden I once asked him, "Why don't you dump the seats?"

"Because it's cheaper than psychiatry," he said.

• • •

The Sunday night ritual was always the same. We drove in under the screeching trolleys of the Lechmere El and parked, two wheels on the sidewalk, on a one-way street in the Italian North End. "Never pay to park," my father said. "It's a matter of principle." We double-timed down the street past cafés with soccer pictures on the wall and espresso urns in the windows, finally entering the Garden on a dark, gum-splotched cement ramp. My father bought a *Record-American* from a newsboy yelling "RECK-ud here . . . Final RECK-ud" and sometimes I bought a thirty-five-cent program. A red-coated usher tore our $2.75 promenade tickets and with hustle and luck we'd be in our seats, five rows behind the goal judge, before organist John Kiley struck the opening bars of *"Paree"* as the Bruins took to the ice.

Kiley, who for decades played the organ at Bruins, Celtics and Red Sox games, must have held the world land speed record for the National Anthem. My father once clocked him at 58 seconds from "O say can you see . . ." to ". . . home of the brave." He filled stoppages in play with whatever song he felt like playing until the mid-seventies, when he was required by Garden management to play irrelevant "Charge" calls and other distracting nonsense that is today a staple of so-called "game presentation" in all arenas. But when I first began going to the Garden, dull spots in the action were enlivened by another and better Garden phenomenon — the gallery god. The loudmouthed gods — mostly denizens of the second balcony — were decades ahead of ABC TV Sports in getting "up close and personal."

"Hey, Powers," a gallery god once yelled at the Garden president during a particularly inept Bruin performance, "are you really paying these guys?" To which a second gallery god quickly delivered the punch line: "No, sucker, *you* are."

Bruins Coach Harry Sinden got a typical Garden welcome in 1967, his first season behind the team's bench, when a gallery god apparently felt the Bruins were underachieving: "Harrrreeeee," yelled the god, "there's a bus leaving Park Square at midnight. Be under it."

Don McKenney, a stylish and effective Boston forward from 1954 to 1963, was derisively nicknamed "Mary" because of his perceived reluctance to hit. "Hit him with your purse, Mary," the gods would yell, notwithstanding that McKenney was among the team's top scorers.

The gods showed mercy only to fighters. Perhaps that accounts for the Bruins' long line of contenders for the NHL heavyweight crown: Shore, Fernie Flaman, Teddy Green, Terry O'Reilly. By the late sixties the team was widely known as the Big Bad Bruins—the biggest, roughest, meanest, hardest-partying players in hockey. "Lost the game, won the fight," was the way a generation of gallery gods said, "We got our money's worth."

But none of us ever got our money's worth the way we did on May 10, 1970, when Bobby Orr created the Garden's single most dramatic moment. In the fourth game of the Stanley Cup finals, with Boston leading St. Louis three games to none and the game tied 3-3 in sudden death overtime, Orr took a Derek Sanderson pass from the right corner, cut around defenseman Noel Picard, shot the puck past goalie Glenn Hall and then took a celebratory bellyflop, the dive preserved forever by the lens of photographer Ray Lussier in what would become hockey's most famous photograph — the supreme player in his supreme moment.

Over the years I came to think of Boston Garden the way Holly Golightly thought of Tiffany's in Truman Capote's *Breakfast at Tiffany's:* that "Nothing very bad could happen to you there." Others apparently felt differently.

By the mid-seventies there was growing criticism of the building, with its 588 obstructed-view seats, poor acoustics, inadequate restrooms, insufficient parking (even my father was paying to park by the seventies) and what was widely perceived as the general seediness of the place. Sightings of rats and mice were common.

In 1996 the old Garden was replaced by one of those big, bright, architecturally antiseptic arenas complete with gleaming escalators, huge concourses, cushy club seats, a massive Jumbotron, numerous and capacious restrooms, even more numerous and pricey concessions stands and corporate luxury boxes which, for all I know, are arranged in the *Fortune* 500 order of finish. The new place stops short of being vulgar. But forty-seven percent of its 17,565 seats would have been *outside* of the confines of the Boston Garden. You can see a game in the new arena, but you can't participate. I don't go there very often and when I do go, about the only thing that reminds me of the old Garden is the spoked B logo on the Bruins' shirts and the fact that the organist still plays *"Paree"* when the team takes the ice for warmups and games.

Driven by a nostalgic curiosity, I tried to look up *"Paree"* among the music reference books at the local library but found nothing. I asked several older Bruins fans about the song's origins or lyrics, but they seemed only vaguely aware of it being played and knew nothing about it. Even the Bruins' public relations department could not answer my request for the lyrics. But recently, when I went to a local hardware store to buy new fencing for my backyard rink, I ran into Rene Rancourt, the dapper, tuxedoed French-Canadian who for twenty years has been singing "The Star-Spangled Banner" and "O Canada" before Bruins games. I asked him if he knew anything about the song. "Oh, that's a very obscure song," he said, pausing, then softly and tentatively humming a bar before looking away, seemingly distracted. Then without warning he broke into a full-volume rendition of the French lyrics right there beside the cash register at Town Paint and Supply on South Main Street. *"PARIS, Reine du monde/ Paris, c'est une blonde . . . ."* But that was apparently all he knew. "I think I have the music at home. I'll send it to you," he said to the apparent relief of the cashier. Later that day I turned on my telephone answering machine and there was Rene singing Jose Padilla's English lyrics (which are not a translation of the French) to the 1928 march by Lucien Boyer and Jacques Charles. " *Paree,* I still adore you/ *Paree,* I'm longing for you . . ." I laughed out loud and saved the tape to play for Barbara.

• • •

My last look at the old Garden came in 1998, when I took an eighty-year-old aunt to the new arena for a concert by the Andre Rieu Johann Strauss Orchestra. Before the concert we went to dinner at a North End restaurant. As we walked down Causeway Street we came to what was left of the Garden. The building had been disemboweled like a picador's horse in a bull ring. A demolition crew had ripped down the East wall, allowing a clear view of the building's innards; loose wires and twisted steel reinforcing rods hung down everywhere. Most of the seats were still in place. I pressed up against a temporary chain link fence and looked down to the arena's west end, behind where the net would be, and counted back five rows, then counted three and four seats in from the right-hand aisle: Section G, Row E, Seats 3 and 4. It was the last time I saw the place. It was rush hour and commuters hurried past heading for the trains moving out of the North Station. A few stopped to lean against the fence and stare into the partially demolished building. I don't know what they were thinking. But I suppose the response would be similar to the feeling you'd get walking past the house of an old flame: the depth of feeling would depend on the depth of the former relationship.

"What a mess," my aunt said.

"I loved that place," I said, though not directly to her.

It was only later, as I sat half-listening to the concert — and fantasizing about a gallery god informing Mr. Rieu that there was a bus leaving from Park Square at midnight (information from which some of us might have profited) — that my mind wandered to the adjacent wreckage of the old Garden and to the wonderful times I'd had there. The grave-digging scene from *Hamlet* came to mind: *Alas, poor Yorick! I knew him, Horatio: A fellow of infinite mirth . . . he hath borne me on his back a thousand times and now how abhorred in my imagination it is.*

As for the new arena, I agree with what a *New York Times* writer said in 1924 on the occasion of the closing of New York's old Madison Square Garden: "The new [place] is going to have to be warmed by some historic sporting moments before anyone can rest assured that it is a worthy successor."

• • •

It was shortly after seven o'clock on the morning of Sunday, January 16, 2000, and snow was less than a half hour away when my daughter Tracey, who'd been visiting for the weekend, came downstairs carrying her son Demetre Justis (Digger) Fontaine, age five months, one week, six days.

"Would you mind if I took Digger skating?" I asked. "I'll just carry him around. We'll only be five minutes."

"Taaaaake yooooouuuur tiiiiiime," she said in a way that suggested her son's quizzical smile and vigorous two-legged kicking reflected an early-morning joy and energy not shared by his mother. Tracey was soloing on child care that weekend since her husband was working. Notwithstanding that my son-in-law has one of the great hockey names of all time — Maurice Henri Fontaine, those first two names so reminiscent of the Montreal Canadiens' legendary Richard brothers, Maurice "the Rocket" and Henri "the Pocket Rocket" — my son-in-law was a basketball player and, judging from the size of my grandson's hands and feet, he, too, is likely to be a hoopster. Still, one should be exposed to all of one's sporting options.

While I laced up my skates, Tracey zipped Digger, still smiling and kicking, into a red one-piece, pointy-hooded coat that left only his face exposed. Like most babies, his chubby face, so framed, looked like the face of a small Winston Churchill.

I went out the kitchen door with my grandson held in my left arm and looking over my left shoulder. "Bye, Demetre. Have fun with Grandpa," said Tracey. "Be careful, Dad," she said, in a lower voice.

When we got to the end of the plywood walkway and just before I stepped over the boards onto the ice, I took my grandson off my shoulder and cradled him in both arms as though he were a football and I a running back for whom not fumbling was a higher priority than gaining yardage.

With Mr. Churchill thus protected I took our first careful and tentative strides counterclockwise around the rink. As we came around at the end of the first lap I could see my daughter watching us through the kitchen window. But by the time we came around again, Tracey had been lured away, probably by the smell of fresh-brewed coffee and the promising sight of the huge *Boston Sunday Globe.* Mr. Churchill had stopped smiling, but he was still kicking his legs alternately as if riding an invisible unicycle. I took this to be an expression of unbounded enthusiasm and repositioned him to my right arm, again tucking him away like a football, only this time one carried by a running back sprinting down the sidelines while a TV commentator shouts, "He's holding that ball like a loaf of bread. This is a fumble waiting to happen!"

We circled the rink faster. Mr. Churchill kicked harder. I wondered idly if, seven or eight years hence, I might ask Mr. Churchill if he'd done his homework. I wondered if he'd know the answer.

We continued skating even as the first snowflakes fell. I cannot truly say I whistled or sang or hummed to my grandson, because I cannot do those things in any sort of tuneful way. But what I *can* do is reproduce a song in my head exactly as I might hear it on an album or in concert. And as

I swept around the rink with my grandson on my arm I began adjusting my stride so that I was skating in time with the music in my imagination, which is where the late John Kiley was sitting at his Boston Garden organ and the strains of *"Paree"* echoed again in the arena of my mind and the last two lines of the lyrics I had just learned ran through my head: *You know I left my heart with you/ Although I said adieu.*

Of True Worth and Tomato Stakes

We don't have a stick rack at the Bacon Street Omni, so we we line up our hockey sticks along the back porch wall to the left of the kitchen door and to the right of a blue plastic milk crate filled with pucks. There are at any time in the skating season ten to fifteen sticks of various lengths and blade curvatures (some of which even conform to NHL rules) lined up against the wall. Barbara and I routinely tell friends and visitors to help themselves to sticks and pucks if they feel like skating when neither of us is home or if they don't have sticks of their own.

In the winter of 1984-85 one of Wayne Gretzky's sticks stood against that wall. I know I was the only one in the family to use it because I'm the only one in the immediate family who shoots left, as does Gretzky. I suspect that some of our left-shooting friends may have used it a few times when we weren't home. I hope they did and I hope they didn't show it any more reverence than they'd show any of the other sticks along that wall. I hope this because of what I learned from my late father years ago. It was a lesson in the economics of true worth and it began with a note he left on the kitchen table.

I saw the note at 5:30 on a weekday morning when, still rubbing sleep out of my eyes, I came downstairs to grab a quick breakfast before starting out on my morning paper route (I had a modest start in the journalism business).

"Another tribute to my cat-like reflexes," read the note in my father's bold script. My father phrased things that way.

The note was weighted down by an official National Hockey League Art Ross autograph model game puck. My first hockey souvenir. I figured my father had caught it at the Boston Bruins vs. Chicago Blackhawks game at Boston Garden the night before. I picked up the puck and examined it. Clearly this was an object to be kept and revered. Here was a tangible connection, a bridge, between me and my late-1950s hockey heroes. Had Johnny Bucyk's skate ripped that little chunk of rubber out of the puck's rim? Had the tape on Stan Mikita's stick left that skid mark across the orange label? Had the entire puck once been enclosed in Chicago goalie Glenn Hall's glove?

Later, at supper, my father told of his bare-handing of a Bobby Hull slapper as the puck clipped the top of the glass and sailed into the stands. Then he told the truth. The puck had squirted up out of a crowd of players, toppled over what was then a low wall of protective glass, and landed in my father's friend's cup of beer. No matter. I was like a scientist with a moon rock, repeatedly turning the puck over in my hands, examining every inch of it, marveling at this object that had come from a place I could only dream of going.

We didn't have a fireplace and thus didn't have a mantle on which to display the puck. So I decided to take it to the

sanctus sanctorum of my room — the top shelf of my book-
case — where I could admire it daily. When my father saw
the puck there he said something I understood intuitively at
the time but intellectually only many years later. "You ough-
ta throw that thing in your hockey bag," he said. "Someday
you'll be glad you have it."

By the time he said that, the novelty of the puck had worn
off and it had already become part of the unnoticed background of my room just like the pile of comic books, the college pennants and a stack of baseball cards held together
with a rubber band. Later that winter, I tossed it into the old
Army duffle that served as my hockey bag. Just as a backup.
Just in case we got up to Long Pond and lost all the pucks.
Or someone forgot to bring a puck. That happened. And a
lot more than it should have.

Predictably, there came a day when my souvenir was the
only puck left. Just as predictably, we lost it. It came on one
of those late winter days, when errant passes went sliding
into the water on the north shore of the pond where the sun
was already melting the ice. We lost so many pucks that my
NHL puck was the only one left. I threw it out onto the ice.
It was in play for about five minutes and has, as far as I
know, rested at the bottom of the pond ever since. But the
only thing that bothered me about losing that puck was that
its loss meant we were reduced to playing hockey with a
chunk of wood. Whatever my original fascination with that
NHL puck had been, it vanished completely once we played
hockey with it. Perhaps I discovered a corollary to the old
Groucho Marx line: How could I respect a puck that would

have me as a player? But more likely, I'd come to fully grasp my father's message: that the worth and beauty of an object lies not in the object itself but in its utility — in the pen writing, the brush painting, the puck skimming goalward.

That philosophy is as egalitarian as it is utilitarian. I applaud the professional player's skill, celebrate his triumphs, rejoice in his mastery of the game. But I feel uncomfortable watching professional collectors beg players for pucks and souvenirs, panhandle them for broken sticks, ambush them for autographs in what amount to hotel lobby stakeouts or — more repulsive by far — pay for autographs at those insipid trading card and memorabilia shows.

In the winter of 1984-85 I spent about two weeks with Wayne Gretzky and the then-Stanley Cup champion Edmonton Oilers, to research a magazine cover story on Gretzky, the writing of magazine pieces being a facet of journalism far more lucrative — though less bucolic — than a morning paper route. I'd filed the story on a Sunday night after a game in New Jersey and I stopped by the Oilers' Monday morning practice to thank Gretzky and some of the other players for their cooperation. As I headed out the dressing room door, Gretzky called me back.

"You shoot left?" he asked.

I said I did and he gave me one of his sticks. I appreciated the stick, but not as much as the question that suggested exactly what Gretzky intended I do with that stick. The same thing he'd do. Use it.

I caught a late morning flight home and by mid-afternoon I was out on the backyard rink using Gretzky's stick in a pickup game with kids from the neighborhood. It was a good stick. Light. Strong. It survived the backyard rink season and held together for a few games of spring driveway hockey before someone inevitably stepped on the blade, whereupon I threw it in a corner of the garage with all the other broken sticks.

In June I did the same thing with Gretzky's stick that I did with twenty-three other bladeless shafts. I hammered it into the soft ground of the garden and staked a tomato plant to it. There was Gretzky's Titan (he'd later switch to Easton and then to Hespeler sticks after he bought a piece of the latter company) amidst the Kohos, Christians, Louisvilles and the brand we've named the tomato patch for — Sher-Wood, as in Sher-Wood Forest.

The hockey stick, of course, ranks just behind the wheel and the knife in any listing of the most useful tools devised by mankind. And for all I know Gretzky's stick may have been one of the many broken ones I've used over the years for cleaning gutters, removing hot grill covers, propping open car hoods, beating rugs, hoisting Christmas lights onto hooks, knocking pears and apples off trees, scraping snow off windshields, or any of the other myriad household uses a hockey stick is good for.

Like any other stick, Gretzky's lasted about three or four years before it gave way to rot, termites and general abuse. I eventually threw it away. But in so doing neither I nor the termites did Gretzky's stick any irreverence. We were — as my father would have said — glad to have had it.

The Jacket

It is one of those old-fashioned hockey jackets from the sixties and I'd sometimes wear it while working on the backyard rink digging postholes, shoveling the ice or even resurfacing on a night that wasn't too cold. It doesn't fit me any more, but unlike the other old designated "rink coats" I've destroyed and discarded over the years, this particular jacket is now in comfortable retirement in a garment bag in my cellar. About once a year I zip open the garment bag and look in on the jacket. Just to make sure it's still there. Still intact. Then I'll take it off its hanger and slip it on just for a few seconds. I don't think I'll ever throw it out. It stands for something.

• • •

The wonder of an old team jacket should be that it warms you twice: once by wrapping you in body heat, and again by enfolding you in the crest and colors that bring back warm memories. But for years this old hockey jacket chilled me with embarrassment.

This jacket may represent the high-water mark of excessive hero worship of a sports star by an adolescent. The *sight* of this jacket so embarrassed me that for years I kept it hidden in a plastic bag under the cellar stairs. Once in a while, primed by a wave of nostalgia (in turn, primed by a couple of beers), I might wear it on the rink. But always when I was alone. I never wore it where someone might see it and laugh at me.

Yet I couldn't bring myself to throw the jacket away or to abandon it when it almost fell victim to one of Barbara's cellar-cleaning frenzies. "But . . . but . . . it's just so inexplicably stupid," Barbara said after I had declined her invitation to pitch the jacket into a trash bag.

Stupid? Yes. I'll also plead guilty to pretentious, impulsive and immature. But the act was not inexplicable. I can and will explain it.

• • •

It is late March of 1962 and the twenty members of St. Mary's CYO hockey team of Winchester, Massachusetts are gathered in the parish hall to be measured for the jackets that are our reward for an undefeated season. We stand in line in front of a salesman who measures us and then writes down the name or nickname we want stitched on the left sleeve. It is my turn.

"Thirty-four inches," the salesman mutters, scribbling my sleeve length on his order pad.

"Name? Spell, please," he says.

I start to spell my name, "J . . . A . . . C . . . " and then I make my mistake. But I have help. "Q . . . U . . . E . . . S," yells out one of my teammates from somewhere near the back of the line. Others laugh. I laugh. It's an inside joke. The "Jacques" my teammate refers to is, of course, Jacques Plante, the great goaltender for the Montreal Canadiens and, as everyone on the team knows, my one and only sports hero.

Sure, I think. Why not? Aren't I the team's goaltender? Doesn't my admiration for Plante go so far that I have even tried to ape the man's roving style of play—with absolutely no discernible success except that people have yelled at me, as they did at Plante, "Get back in your [bleeping] net." Didn't I sometimes wear a towel around my neck, à la Plante, in pre-game warmups? (Jacques and I knew we had the game's first throat protectors.) Wasn't mine an admittedly blatant case of all-out hero worship? Why not, indeed?

"J . . . A . . . C . . . Q . . . U . . . E . . . S," I say. I laugh. All around me teammates are breaking up. Good joke.

Bad move.

The enormity of the mistake is made clear to me a month later when I take delivery of a jacket that has someone else's name on the sleeve. And a French name at that. And, even worse, the name of a superstar. Pretentious? No more so than a light-hitting rec league softball player having "Babe" or "Yaz" stitched on his team jacket. A player wouldn't do that even if his name *were* Babe or Yaz . . . or Jacques.

I felt uncomfortable wearing the jacket. Too many quizzical looks and involved explanations. "No, it's not my name, see, it's Jacques Plante's and he's a goalie for Montreal and . . . ." It was easier to give the jacket early retirement.

• • •

It is Thursday, February 27, 1986, and I am still on early-morning cruise control — moving and thinking at half speed — as I walk into the kitchen while absentmindedly riffling through the morning newspaper. The story woke me up in a hurry. "Jacques Plante died," I said to Barbara, and then I read aloud the report that said Plante had died of stomach cancer at a hospital near his home in the Valais, Switzerland.

Brian walked into the kitchen in time to hear me read the last few paragraphs of the story. Maybe just to humor me or to make conversation he asked if I thought Plante was the greatest goalie ever. I wanted to say yes but instead I gave him the most honest answer I could: "He may not have been the greatest, but he was the most important," I said.

In the weeks after his death, I reflected on Plante's contributions to goaltending and on my long fascination with the man. Even without his introduction of the revolutionary roving style, or his popularization of the goalie mask or his advocacy of goalie coaches — unheard-of back then — Plante's records and statistics alone mark him as one of the greatest goalies ever. He won a record seven Vezina Trophies (then awarded to the goalie allowing the fewest goals), and he won the Hart Trophy as league MVP in 1962, something no other goalie did until Buffalo's Dominik Hasek in 1997 and '98. His name is inscribed six times on the Stanley Cup. He recorded a glittering 2.37 average in 837 regular-season games and an even better 2.16 in 112 play-off games. In his era only fellow Hall of Famers Terry Sawchuk (103) and Glenn Hall (84) had more shutouts than Plante (82).

But Plante had more than talent. He had genius. He was a virtuoso and a stylist who, finding it insufficient merely to master one of the toughest positions in sport, went out and recreated it in his own flamboyant image. Others fiddled with the interior decoration — the style—of goaltending; Plante changed the architecture.

Plante shattered what for decades had been the First Commandment of Goaltending — thou shalt not bother a puck that is not bothering you — in favor of leaving his net to intercept passes and gain possession for his defensemen. Goalies were supposed to wait for trouble and then deal with it as best they could. Thanks to Plante, today's goalies can stop trouble before it happens, but as with most inno-vations, Plante's wanderings were not well received.

"Reveille-toi! Wake up!" Montreal fans would yell at him on those rare occasions when his roamings would result in a goal against the Canadiens. In 1960, when a cranky knee led to an early-season slump, Plante was booed by Forum fans. "After seven years all they see are my saves, not my work," he said. "I play pro hockey; I know what it is like. But most of them, they played school hockey. What do they know?"

As that imperious response suggests, Plante had the air of a haughty sommelier secure in his knowledge of the wine list and contemptuous of the opinions of The Great Unwashed. What *do* they know, indeed? Today, a goalie who cannot handle the puck cannot expect to make a good bantam team.

And then there was the mask. Except for a brief experiment by Clint Benedict in 1929, NHL goalies did not wear masks because 1) it was viewed by teammates and coaches as a tacit admission of fear, and 2) the mask was thought to interfere with the goalie's vision.

Plante rejected both points. "The pleasure of the game is to like [playing], not to think about getting hurt," he said, to which he later amended the rhetorical: "If you jump out a plane without a parachute, does it make you brave?"

In the mid-fifties he started wearing a mask in practice. The mask was partly his own design and had a lot of open space around the eyes so Plante could see the puck clearly.

No matter. Montreal Coach Toe Blake disliked the mask and wouldn't let Plante wear it in games. The breakthrough came on November 1, 1959. Early in the first period of a game against New York at Madison Square Garden, the Rangers' Andy Bathgate smashed Plante's nose with a backhand shot. In those days, NHL teams didn't carry spare goalies. The substitute was supplied by the home team and, in this case, that sub would have been a Madison Square Garden TV technician named Joe Schaefer.

In the dressing room, where Plante's nose was being stitched, Blake asked his goalie if he could go back into the game. Plante said he'd play, but only if he could wear his mask. Blake gave in to the squeeze play, and that night the man who would thereafter be known as The Masked Marvel led the Canadiens to a 3-1 win. Today, any goalie at any level who steps in front of a cage without a mask is considered bereft of his senses.

A player who defies coaches, fans and tradition is, clearly, a player who trusts himself. But the obverse of that self-trust was that Plante did not trust anyone else. At least that was the impression I got the one time I met the man.

It was April 1984 and I was on assignment for *Sports Illustrated* covering a divisional semifinal playoff between Montreal and Quebec. Plante was serving as goalie coach for Montreal and had the Canadiens' rookie goalie Steve Penney playing like a possible playoff MVP. On Wednesday, April 18, Penney had shut out Quebec 4-0 in Quebec City. I returned to Montreal with the Canadiens immediately after the game, and it was well past midnight when I got on the elevator at my hotel, Le Manoir LeMoyne. The only other people in the elevator car were Plante and his Swiss-born wife, Raymonde. Plante and I nodded. He had seen me in the dressing room earlier that night and I had asked him some questions at an informal press conference, but we had never been introduced.

I've never asked an athlete or coach for an autograph — it alters the working relationship — but I thought about making an exception for Plante. I wanted the autograph. Then I looked at it from Plante's point of view. He would have liked the asking but not the asker. I kept my pen in my pocket. But I felt the need to say something. With Montreal ahead three games to two in a best-of-seven series and with Penney playing spectacularly, I speculated (correctly as it turned out) that Penney and Montreal would eliminate Quebec in the next game. "He'll wrap it up Friday," I said to Plante and then added — I don't know why other than as some kind of throwaway line — "if his friends don't let him down."

Plante said nothing. The elevator arrived at his floor. The door slid open and Jacques put his arm in front of it, holding it back while Raymonde stepped off. Then he stepped out, and with his arm still holding back the door, smiled and said, "A goalie has no friends. Good night." The door slid shut.

Was that a joke or did Plante really think that way? I don't know. But what I do know, from all I've heard and read in my forty-plus-year obsession with the man, is that he was not one to seek friends or curry favor. Or, as his ex-Montreal teammate Bernie (Boom Boom) Geoffrion once told me, "Oh, that Plante. He was a very good goalie, eh? But he don't go to no parties."

Plante once told a reporter: "No, I never make friends, not in hockey nor elsewhere, not since I was a teenager. What for? If you are close to someone you must be scheduling yourself to please them."

Yet his own found him. There are NHL goalies past and present to whom Plante was more than friend, he was a mentor. As goalie coach for the Philadelphia Flyers from 1976 to 1982, Plante coached the magnificent Bernie Parent in 1978-79, Parent's last season. His place as one of the game's greats already secure, Parent could easily have resented Plante or rejected his coaching. I once asked Parent how he felt about Plante.

"Before, I just play by instinct," said Parent. "Now Jacques has me thinking and handling the puck more. Now, I don't just react. I know what I am doing."

We were in the visitors' dressing room in the old Boston Garden and Parent was getting dressed while he talked to me. As I started to leave, Parent reached out and jabbed a pudgy finger at my notebook. "You put down there that he was the tops. The best. The [bleeping] best," he said.

I wrote it down.

Shortly after he broke into the league with Buffalo, goalie Tom Barrasso showed me his copy of Plante's book, *Goaltending* (Collier Macmillan Canada, Ltd., 1972). The book was dog-eared, tattered and falling apart, said Barrasso, because he had read it so many times.

And when in 1985, shortly before his cancer was diagnosed, the St. Louis Blues hired Plante as goalie coach, an ecstatic Rick Walmsley, one of the Blues' goalies, said that being coached by Plante would be "like being able to go to a library and take out every book ever written about playing goal."

But shortly after he joined the Blues, Plante complained of not feeling well. He was tested in a St. Louis hospital and the cancer was discovered. He went home to Switzerland to die.

I have thought about Plante a lot since his death. I still think that having his name stitched on my jacket was a stupid thing to do. But I also decided a few years ago that it was time to haul the old jacket out of the garment bag — to come out of the closet, so to speak. The jacket fits well through the arms, which are still thirty-four inches long, but less well around an expanding waistline. I squeeze into it once a year in a kind of private ceremony. I think next year I may make it a point to wear it on the rink at least once. And if anyone notices the name on the left sleeve I'll simply tell them the truth: that Jacques Plante was a man I greatly admired.

If one is to have only one sports hero in life, then one should choose him carefully. I think Jacques was and remains a worthy choice. I'm proud of that.

Rinks and Writing

I began writing about hockey in the tenth grade, and by my senior year of high school my decision to enter college as a journalism major with the intention of pursuing a career in sportswriting had sent legions of relatives, teachers and guidance counselors into fits of hand-wringing despair. Even among professional journalists, sportswriting is regarded as the toy department of any publication. Or, as *Sports Illustrated* writer Frank Deford once said upon receiving one of his many awards as the nation's top sportswriter, "Being the best sportswriter is like being the world's tallest midget."

But we all have to find our own answer to the most fundamental question of life, that being, as Emerson put it: "How are we to earn a blameless livelihood?" To which essayist John Burroughs later appended an even tougher requirement — by means "congenial to our nature."

The chronicling of sports events and profiling of players may be "blameless" enough (although sports talk radio "journalists" and some tabloid columnists are going to have to throw their cases upon the mercy of the court), but the larger question is why sportswriting should be congenial to my, or to any middle-aged adult's, nature. I address the issue as much in the spirit of public service as of purgative introspection.

I think my love of hockey has much to do with the black plastic Admiral AM radio that sat on the bottom shelf of my bedside table — the radio that brought in WHDH and announcer Fred Cusick's play-by-play of the Boston Bruins games I started listening to in 1954 during the winter that my mother died of ovarian cancer.

I think I listened partly because those games represented a surcease in the frightening unknowableness of childhood in general and of that dark winter in particular. Thus my affection for the Bruins and for hockey, which endures undiluted to this day, is much as the late novelist Fred Exley described his feelings for the NFL's New York Giants in his book *A Fan's Notes,* those being ". . . no more than the force of a forgotten childhood."

As a child, whether attending a Bruins game or listening to one in the darkness of my room, I never wanted it to end, partly because I loved the pace and the action, partly because I did not know what would come when the action was over. For me, the game has never ended.

In the gloomy years after my mother's death, when grief metastasized and the tensions that beset all families beset ours, hockey became a critical conversational supply line, the one always-open avenue of communication to my father when the discussion of almost any other subject — school, grades, friends, jobs — could leave me vulnerable to criticism or accusatory harangue. Like a good tactician, I protected my supply line, in this case with knowledge. You can't talk about a sport unless you know it, and I made it my business to know hockey. The game was my sword and my shield.

I later lugged that knowledge into adulthood and added to it. It came in handy during the years of my own children's adolescence. While Barbara and I tried to keep the atmosphere in our home lighter and livelier than the atmosphere in the homes we grew up in (Barbara' father died when she was five and her mother did not remarry) there were still times in our family life when hockey — ice and field — provided the surest and safest conversational link to our children. "How was practice today?" "How about those Bruins?" — could always keep a conversation alive until it worked its way to higher and more substantive ground.

The backyard rink also served, at times, as a family life preserver, uniting us in a common project on which everyone's help was needed and willingly given. Even today, when Barbara and I have what sociologists oxymoronically call "adult children," our phone calls and conversations with Brian and Tracey are peppered from October to March with questions about the rink: "How many boards are up? . . . Do you think we'll beat the frost? . . . Cold enough to flood tonight?" And the two most frequently asked questions: "How's the ice?" and "When are you going to buy a freaking snowblower?"

If mankind is divided into participants and observers, then I suppose that being a hockey writer with a rink of my own has allowed me to have a skate in each camp, though that is a mixed blessing. When from 1982 to 1986 I wrote about hockey for a national magazine, I found that the most vexing part of the job was going to team practices and standing on the sidelines watching other people skate. And yet I have always rejected the claim made by many, including some of my friends, that people become sportswriters because they are not good enough to be players. I think it was now-retired *Boston Herald* columnist Tim Horgan who best answered that claim. "To be a sportswriter," he said, "it is necessary to love the writing as much as the sport." Like most writers, I love the "having written" a lot more than I love the writing. But I've always regarded sportswriting as worthy and fulfilling in itself — a legitimate and professional connection to the game; a way of informing and entertaining people who care — and not as a synthetic substitute for playing. When I feel like playing I go out on my rink and play.

These days I teach a college class, Sports Journalism, wherein I repeat Horgan's quotation on the opening day of each semester.

That class is filled with from twelve to twenty students, nearly all of whom have an honest vocational interest in pursuing careers as sportswriters and who support that interest with uncommon drive. I know this because I schedule the class for 8 A.M., a starting time most college students regard as punitively inconsiderate and to be avoided at almost all costs. I don't like starting that early any more than my students do. But I do it so that the class attracts the strongest and most sincere writers — the ones tough enough, driven enough, strong enough to pay the price to get what they want. The unmotivated, the undisciplined, the weak do not take 8 A.M. classes, and on the rare occasions when a few have tried, they haven't lasted long.

The ones who stay the course are an interesting and admirable group who share the culture and language of sport. If I refer to the demanding legwork of reporting as so much "mucking and grinding in the journalistic corners," I don't have to explain what I mean. One of sport's oldest mantras — "You've got to play hurt" — is so much a part of their character that I almost never have a writer use illness as an excuse for a missed assignment or class. Indeed, I once had a student, now a promising young TV sportscaster, sit through a class while holding his left shoulder, which I later learned had been dislocated in an intramural football game the night before. He was on his way to the infirmary. But he went by way of the classroom. If, to paraphrase Deford, even the best would-be sports journalists are academia's tallest midgets, they are oftentimes the toughest and most admirable. And sometimes the most insightful.

Once each semester — toward the end of the term, after we have covered the basic sportswriting formats of game stories, sidebars, features, player profiles and columns — students have an opportunity to write a short first-person essay about their relationship to sport or to sportswriting. I can't recall any students writing that they wanted to be sportswriters because they knew they weren't good enough to earn a living as players. What I read instead are essays on relationships. Stories, much like my own, of sport connecting young people to parents, grandparents, teachers, coaches, friends, opponents, a school, a community. The roots of my students' interest seem to lie slightly less in the joy of playing — though there is plenty of that — and more in the use of sport as a bridge. Sport and sportswriting are important because people and relationships are important. And that is why a backyard rink is important.

One of the most insightful essays I've read about rinks and relationships came not from one of my students but from my daughter Tracey who, a decade ago, wrote her college application essay on the importance of our backyard rink. (And no, I did not help her with it, nor did I know what it was about until after her applications had been mailed). Tracey, who today is a teacher, wanted to major in Early Childhood Education, thus the general theme of her essay had to do with her learning to skate. But the end of that essay addressed the larger and more important subject of friendship and connection.

> . . . By late February the wind has shifted to the southwest and the sun seems to linger too long. It's a sad time.
>
> "We can always go slushing," one of my friends said after we arrived home from school last year to find the ice too soft to skate on. But I think we knew we were kidding ourselves and it would be another year before we were back on the rink. A sadness came over us as we stood there on the muddy edge of the rink saying our silent good-bye to a friend whose visit always seems too short.
>
> Sometimes I think my friends love the rink as much as I do. It's a place for us to come together. Some of my

friends don't even skate but they seem happy sliding around in sneakers or boots, enjoying everyone's company . . .

. . . with my own rink, I've learned — and been able to share — the joyous freedom of skating. But a new goal has emerged [one has to write phrases like that on college essays]. *I want to skate better and to enjoy that freedom even more. But even if I were not to skate again, the good times, friendship, sportsmanship and camaraderie of the backyard rink is something that won't melt in the spring.*

Even a tall midget working in the toy department is ultimately writing about something consequential: the connection among people. To do this is to earn a blameless livelihood in a way that should be congenial to anyone's nature.

Boards

It was about six o'clock in the evening a few days before Christmas and I was wrapping presents in the cellar when the big red truck with the white "Reynolds Electrical" lettered on its sides backed into my driveway. By the time I got to the kitchen, Steve Reynolds — master electrician, nephew-by-marriage and backyard rink builder who lives about two miles across town — was already rummaging through the bottom right-hand drawer of my refrigerator and pulling out the last twelve-ounce can of light beer from among the darker half-quart bottles of Brian's home-brewed ale. A beer, or for that matter a case of beer, was a small and insufficient price to pay for Steve's enormous favor of getting me a wholesale price on the plastic liner for my rink and delivering same to my house about twelve hours ahead of a rapidly advancing cold front.

I went outside with Steve to help him unload the long cardboard box containing the roll of six-mil clear plastic. (If you're a first-time rink builder you'll be astonished at the weight of a roll of plastic.)

We'd pulled the roll halfway out of the truck when I noticed the label on the side of the box: "100 x 60," it read.

"Whoa, Steve, this is sixty wide, I only need forty," I said.

"Sorry, Unc, almost gave you my roll," said Steve, shoving the sixty footer back into the blackness of the truck and pulling out my one hundred-by-forty foot sheet, which we carried like a stretcher into my rink and dropped near the end boards, from which point Brian and I would unroll it, spread it out, staple it to the plywood boards and begin flooding.

"I thought anything wider than forty feet was a custom job-bie," I said. "Get one for you anytime, Unc," said Steve in that self-assured vaguely conspiratorial voice contractors use with clients, the simple message carrying the subtextual hint of vast reservoirs of untapped resources from whom all things are possible but of which the layman need know nothing.

We went back into the kitchen, where Steve finished his beer and I spent a few minutes mentally reconfiguring my rink to see if, next year, I could make it wider. But that would be difficult. My rink is wedged between a property line on one side and a hedge, garage and pine tree on the other. I'm stuck at about a thirty-five-foot width and sixty-foot length.

But Steve's rink, built in 1997 in the disconcertingly warm winter of El Niño ("Hey, Unc, when do we get ice? I'm watching ducks take off and land in my yard," said an exas-perated Steve during a phone call in mid-winter of that year) is about fifty feet wide and roughly seventy feet long. Put it this way: Steve's rink can accommodate a good game of three-on-three with all of the passing and tactical permuta-tions that that implies. And while we can play and have played three-on-three on my rink, the optimal game at the Bacon Street Omni is a more rudimentary two-on-two.

The chief advantages of having your own rink are: convenience, safety, containment of shots and passes, and the assurance that — as long as it stays cold — you'll be able to skate long after the local ponds have been covered with snow or ruined by the footprints of nonskaters or inconsiderate hoseheads who went traipsing over the ice when it was soft and slushy and for whom there should be reserved a special place deep in the infernal Penalty Box. The chief disadvantage of most backyard rinks is limited space. Which is why, on several days this year, I skated on my own rink in the morning and on nearby Little Jennings Pond in the afternoon, something I've done many times before.

I like skating on ponds because the ice surface is large and I am uncorraled by boards. Skimming over a frozen pond I've always felt like the character Sears in John Cheever's *Oh What a Paradise it Seems,* "completely absorbed in the illusion that fleetness and grace were in [my] possession and had only to be revealed." This feeling is familiar only to a diminishing number of skaters who, like me, are old enough to have grown up skating on lakes and ponds before the Bobby Orr-inspired "hockey boom" of the 1970s saw thousands of new rinks built across North America. These are the buildings that brought skating in general and hockey in particular into a neon-lighted benevolent captivity from which it will never escape.

Pushing a puck before me on one late December afternoon, I glided toward the far end of the pond, away from the half dozen or so children, two or three parents and one dog who remained clustered near the shore, probably a safe thing to do when you're skating on lake or pond ice. I skated in huge circles and distorted figure eights, happy to be free of the constraints of boards and the impediment of a hockey goal. I'd skated for about twenty minutes and was sucking wind pretty badly (my enthusiasm being vastly ahead of my conditioning) when I knelt on the ice to take a rest. The late December sun was already well below the jagged horizon of the tree line when I looked back toward the still-open ice where the pond waters run through a culvert under a nearby street and empty into the larger Jennings Pond. A yellow school bus rumbled past, probably filled with hockey or basketball players since this was Christmas vacation week and schools were closed. As I knelt, catching my breath and watching that bus, my thoughts went back to another school bus in another December on another pond.

It was a Friday in December in the mid-1970s and I was coaching the then-second-year varsity hockey team at the Rivers School in Weston, Massachusetts, about three miles from my home in Natick. We were holding our last practice before Christmas break and, with about two weeks until our next game, it was a desultory session, as though the cold and gloom of the town rink had somehow dripped into our spirits. "I can't tell if they're speeding up or slowing down," my assistant coach said during a skating drill.

Players remained subdued as the bus brought us back to school. It had been a 2 to 3 P.M. practice, so there was still plenty of light as the bus pulled up to the front of the gym.

I don't remember who said it, but just before the driver opened the door, a voice from the back of the bus yelled, "There's black ice on Nonesuch."

Several of us turned at once to look out the bus window at Nonesuch Pond on the edge of the school property, about 300 yards from the gym. It was covered with the season's first ice, the so-called "black ice," though strictly speaking, there is no such thing as black ice. The black effect is caused by the perfect transparency of new ice, not yet sullied by admixtures of snow and still thin enough to let the darker color of the pond waters show through.

About seven or eight players — mostly seniors who didn't have to rely on parents for rides home — got off the bus and headed straight for the pond. Players who twenty minutes earlier couldn't wait to stop skating now couldn't wait to start.

That afternoon I abandoned one of the coaching maxims given to me by the school's athletics director. "Never play against your own team," he had said. To which I'd amended, "Especially if the players are a lot better than you are." The thinking there is that credibility is a fragile thing and a playing coach could have a lot to lose. But that thinking is and was wrong. I had much to gain by skating with those kids, and that afternoon I gained it.

Out on the pond, without boards or blue lines or icing rules — constraints my players had grown up with and I had gotten used to — the game took on new dimensions. The bigger, generally rougher players had no corners in which to assert their physical dominance. And careless passes that would normally bounce off the boards of the rink now went sliding hundreds of yards down the ice. We made up a rule: The player making a bad pass, or the player failing to collect a good pass, would have to go retrieve the puck. The rest of us served as judge and jury, and it was pointless to throw yourself at the mercy of a merciless court, to wit:

Player A: "I'm not gettin' that. Morelli didn't even reach for it."

Player B: "He shouldn't have to reach for it, Shaunessy. Go get it before I smack ya."

There weren't many bad passes after the first ten minutes or so.

The open ice demanded and rewarded creativity and we adjusted quickly. Our game gradually spread over a wider area and we improvised plays that were not in our or anybody's playbook. Ours was a game of the creation and use of space—pond hockey the way former Montreal Canadiens goaltender Ken Dryden would describe it five years later in his book *The Game:* "I tried things I had never tried before, my hands and feet discovering new patterns and directions, and came away feeling as if something was finally clear . . . hockey was weaned on long northern winters . . . it grew up on ponds and rivers in big open spaces, unorganized . . . only occasionally moved into arenas for practices and games."

I can't say that we became a better team for having played outdoors for that one transcendent hour. I *can* say that I — that all of us, I think — partook of a different and in some ways better game than the one we'd earlier played in the town rink. We played the game as it was originally intended to be played — creatively, spontaneously and with the emphasis on skating and passing.

Now I don't suggest that we forthwith rip down the rink boards and play the Stanley Cup final on Lake Erie. If the ice is a canvas, it still needs a frame. But in the long-running discussion over whether we North Americans should expand our standard 200-by-85-foot rink in favor of the 200-by-100-foot European rink, I find myself favoring the larger surface. To adopt the larger surface is not so much to change our game but to bring it home.

· · ·

As I finish writing these thoughts I can look out of the den window on my left and see my rink in the early morning light. Again, I do some mental reconfiguring. The truth is I could get about five or six feet closer to that pine tree on the east side. And I could go at least another foot or two wider before encroaching on Mrs. Henriques' yard on the west side.

Next year I may have Steve Reynolds get me that sixty-foot-wide roll of plastic. It's not greed. It's manifest destiny.

When it comes to backyard rinks, size matters.

The Five Truths
of Shoveling

It is snowing hard this morning, a wet snow whipped by a northeast wind and accumulating at about an inch an hour. Street and sidewalk plows will soon push huge slushy chunks of compacted and dirty snow into our driveway where, if I don't remove it quickly, it will harden into a wall of ice that will have to be broken up with a long-handled spade before it can be removed with a snow shovel. I suspect I'll have shoveled my one-car-width driveway at least twice before I turn my attention to the snow accumulating on our rink. There should be eight to twelve inches of it before the storm drifts into the Atlantic tonight.

I could buy a snowblower — or, easier, borrow my neighbor's (who would have an interest in loaning it to me since he and his children occasionally skate on my rink) — and thus eliminate the need for all this rigorous shoveling. When I was in my mid-forties I said I'd buy a snowblower when I turned fifty. But now I'm fifty-five and I've pushed my snowblower target date ahead another three years. I'll buy the snowblower when I'm fifty-eight. Maybe. Until then I'll continue to regard shoveling as an ancillary benefit of the rink, one yielding beneficial exercise in a measurably worthy cause — as distinct, say, from running in place on a treadmill or riding a stationary bicycle to nowhere. I don't belong to a gym, but in the fall and winter I probably get more exercise than most men my age and the rink accounts for a lot of it. Digging postholes, wrestling the boards into place, shoveling and skating burn a lot of calories from October to March, the health benefit of which was memorably observed three years ago when a physician's assistant visited my house to administer a cursory physical for an insurance policy I was buying. I could tell from his accent that he was from somewhere in eastern Europe and could tell by his demeanor that he was distracted and in a hurry. After drawing two blood samples — an act that alone figured to send my blood pressure soaring — he slapped on the blood pressure cuff, pumped the little bulb, looked at the gauge and grunted. The grunt had me worried. Then he whipped out a stethoscope and listened to my heart. He grunted again, appeared to listen harder, then muttered, more to himself than to me, "Like a Sviss vatch."

Having never owned a Swiss watch, I can only hope those chronometers deserve their reputations as strong and enduring instruments.

But the moral lessons of the snow shovel supersede the physical benefits. Here are five truths I've learned in seventeen years of shoveling snow off of my rink:

1. There are only three kinds of people.

First are the folks who will help you shovel your rink without being asked. Then you have the vast majority who will help you shovel if you ask them to. Alas, Emerson was right when he wrote that the highest price we can pay for anything is to ask for it, so I have little experience with this group. Last and ignobly least are the people who would prefer a root canal or hip replacement to helping you (or anyone) shovel snow.

You don't have to run a backyard rink for too many years before you see the truth behind the old line that sport doesn't build character, it reveals it. Many — and uncharitably remembered — are the skaters who won't call for ice conditions until at least forty-eight hours after the passing of a major snowstorm on the off chance that there might still be snow on the rink and the even more unlikely chance that we will ask them to help shovel it. And then there is Smitty.

It was about six o'clock on a winter morning a few years ago when Barbara and I awoke to a sound on our back porch. Our son was away at college and our daughter was asleep upstairs, so the noise didn't come from either of them. I went out to the back door to investigate and there on the porch found our son Brian's friend Chris Smith, who was just coming home from his job as a police dispatcher and had stopped at our house to shovel a four-inch overnight snowfall off our rink. He was grabbing one of the three shovels we keep on the porch.

"Stealing shovels again, Smitty?" I said.

"Nah, I thought I'd knock this snow off the rink. Didn't mean to wake you up."

Had we not heard him I think he would have cleared the entire rink by himself. Instead, I put on a pot of coffee and went out to help him. It was a light snow and I think we cleared it in about a half hour, at which point Barbara was in the process of making a huge stack of blueberry pancakes.

Later that morning Brian's friend Matt Adams called to see if we needed help shoveling. Matt, like Smitty, will rank high in any listing of *Snow Tonnage Shoveled - Career* should I ever publish a *Bacon Street Omni Media Guide and Record Book.*

I'm grateful to Matt, Smitty, Keith Fleming and others who have grabbed a shovel, marched to the front and performed vigorously. Their willing generosity reflects well on them. And on their parents.

As for that third group . . . well, the shirkers we shall have always with us. But I don't think about them much. It is enough that I know who they are and that, in their hearts, they know I know. Paradoxically, while I credit the parents of the Smittys and the Matts and others like them, I don't blame the parents of the shirkers. Shirking is a reaction. Shoveling is a choice.

2. Look back and take heart.

The older I get the more likely I am to reinforce my motivation for shoveling not by looking ahead at the snow I have yet to tie into but by looking back at the ice I've already cleared.

Shoveling is hard work, and while you're doing it you have to concentrate on what's in front of you, which too often can be several hundred cubic feet of snow. But no one can shovel for long without taking a few seconds' rest to let the heart rate drop and to regain energy. During these pauses I used to stare at the unbroken field of snow before me, redoubling my resolve to remove it; to roll up the enemy's front and flanks, smash him up and drive him from the field into the garden and onto the side lawn. Mine was the George Patton - Ulysses Grant philosophy of snow removal: Relentless attack. So deeply ingrained is this military approach to shoveling that a few years ago, when Barbara and I were removing a snowfall so heavy that we decided to do only half the rink one day and finish it the next, I shoveled an equator across the middle of the rink and called back to Barb, "Hey, Caesar, stop when you get to the Rubicon." Not unlike the Roman general, Barb smiled and said, "We'll see." We stayed out an extra hour and finished the job.

In the last few years, when I stop to lean on my shovel and take stock of things, I'm more inclined to look at the beckoning expanse of cleared and inviting ice behind me or even to stare up at the evergreens or into the hedge and listen to the chickadees and other birds of winter. I'm no longer preoccupied with work and the time required to do it. Being goal-directed is a useful thing. "Eyes on the prize," is a worthy slogan. But you can also find motivation and renewal in looking at what you've done and enjoying where you are.

3. To start is to be half done.

The mythical sword of Damocles, hanging by a hair over the head of that yapping Dionysian courtier, was probably only a little more disconcerting than is the snow shovel leaning on the back porch wall as snow piles up on the ice. Sword and shovel are weighty with portentousness. The job of clearing the rink hangs heavy on my mind. But only when I'm not doing it. And in this it is much like a piece of writing. A college writing professor told me thirty-five years ago that the hardest part of any story is starting it. "Start and you're half done," he said and he was practically — if not mathematically — correct. The same professor also told me not to wait for inspiration before I write, but to begin writing and the inspiration would find me. It is the same with shoveling or with any big job. Once I'm on the rink and snow is flying and clean ice is appearing and the battle is fairly joined, then my thoughts turn from the fatiguing weight of work undone to a preoccupation with the vigorous prosecution of the war on my archenemy, snow.

And the main trick I use to get me to the snow shovel is the same one I use to bring me to the writing desk: I decide a particular time for starting and ending. The starting time is sacrosanct. Once that decision is made only the most dire emergency can prevail against it. If I decide I'll start shoveling at 5 P.M. then that's it. There is no choice or stalling or flexibility, because I don't want to get into the business of lying to myself since I think that's something that would get progressively easier to do.

But once the shoveling has begun, the stop time — for shoveling, writing or any other job — gets pushed up. I almost always shovel longer than I'd planned to and leave the rink with the satisfaction that comes not with meeting the goal but exceeding it.

4. You need a plan.

Divide and conquer works for me. My rink is about thirty-five feet wide, but I don't open the war by fighting along a thirty-five foot front. I concentrate my forces.

Were I to work my way across the entire width of the rink, progress would not only *seem* slow but would actually *be* slow because of the need to carry snow from the middle of the rink to the boards before dumping it. So instead I divide the snow into sections, first driving my entering wedge lengthwise down the middle of the rink, then dividing each half into thirds, thus creating six comparatively small sections. I then attack each section, pushing the snow from the middle of the ice toward the boards until I get to a point where I can use the shovel to pitch the snow directly out of the rink. (Barbara says her approach is different: "I don't think. I shovel.") Progress is fast and encouraging when I fall into that scoop-throw, scoop-throw rhythm that fills the air with superfine snow particles that blow back off the shovel and cling to my eyebrows and sparkle in the light.

The hardest part of the job is pitching the snow over the four-foot-high boards at one end of the rink. But by the time I work my way to that end the job is almost done, and I find the same kind of extra energy one finds in the last few yards of a long run. I plan it this way.

5. It makes the ice new again.

That is the final and essential truth of shoveling. New ice is always a joy.

Metaphors

It was on one of the few skating days in the eerily warm winter of El Niño in 1997 that I looked out the kitchen window to see my daughter Tracey skating alone, swooping around the backyard rink on old skates, the boots and blades of which were marked with the dings, scars and tears of hockey games past. Unlike the rest of us — Barbara, Brian, me or almost anyone else who uses the rink — Tracey rarely puts the net in place. The big steel-framed goal remained tilted upside-down over the low boards where, the night before, I'd wrestled it off of the rink so I could resurface the ice.

I've got the goal frame draped with an old tennis net, and much of the fun of skating on the rink is blasting a puck or tennis ball into the netting and watching it balloon out as did the loosely draped goals shown in old hockey photographs. And anyone who bulges the netting without imagining he is scoring a goal in the NHL is lying, unimaginative or a terminal grown-up.

But Tracey, on that morning as on so many other times when I'd watched her skate, was content merely to stick-handle, which she did while turning now this way and suddenly that way, swerving, pivoting and taking off in new and unforseeable directions. Once in a while she'd shoot. But not often.

She is different from her mother. Barbara drives to the net with a choppy, wide-tracking, ice-gouging stride, her course always full speed ahead, her body pitched dangerously forward, forever on the edge of control and always driven by a will that vastly exceeds her modest skating ability.

Give Barbara the puck in a pickup game and chances are you won't get it back. Barbara wouldn't pass the ketchup. She just goes to the net. But give Tracey the puck, and somehow or other it will come back to you — saucered over a stick, banked off a board, threaded through a forest of legs — most likely arriving on your stick blade when you least expect it. I think the difference in their styles is not merely the difference between mother and daughter but between two wholly different generations of women athletes, the older woman aggressively seizing the beachhead of athletic opportunity, the younger woman using that beachhead as a staging area for the drive toward greater skill and achievement.

That difference is one I first noticed not on the ice but on the fields. And with that recognition came another truth I still find darkly portentous.

• • •

An apple is autumn made edible, and none evoked memories of boyhood autumns — days redolent of burning leaves and the cider press — more than the small, cool McIntoshes

I took from the bottom of the bin at Cicarelli's Bacon Street Farm, for many years my last stop on the way to Natick (Massachusetts) High School field hockey games.

The girls thought the three dozen Macs I left near the bench in a brown paper bag were a gift. A post-game snack. That was only partly true. The apples were my cover.

At first I didn't know a parent needed a cover to go to field hockey games. But that was before I learned the two Great Truths of that sport: 1) hardly anyone goes to high school field hockey games, and 2) every ten seconds an official blows a whistle whether the game needs one or not. I exaggerate only a little.

"Hi, Dad, what are you doing here?" Tracey asked that September years ago when she spotted me prowling the sidelines of the team's first game and her first start. I didn't expect the question and don't remember my answer. I do remember driving to a nearby store and returning with two cello-wrapped packages of apples. "Brought you girls some apples," I said, hoping the offering would somehow justify my presence and deflect what I thought were the curious glances of players not used to seeing parents at away games.

I couldn't answer Tracey's question because I did not truly know why I was there. The best answer I might have come up with is that I was drawn by a parent's apprehensive curiosity as to how my daughter would do playing my wife's sport.

As a high school star of at least the second magnitude, my wife was the leading scorer and two-time letter winner at Northampton, Massachusetts, High School in the early sixties. When Barbara talks about that — which is seldom — she often refers to herself as a "tomboy," as though her ability to play a sport hard and well somehow pushed her to the fringes of the social mainstream. But in eight years of watching more than one hundred of our daughter's high school and college field hockey games, I never heard Tracey or any of her teammates use that word. If "tomboy" came up on their Scholastic Aptitude Tests they probably got it wrong. They called themselves "players" and "athletes," and that is what I called them, and they are the first generation of female athletes wholly at ease with their athleticism.

I also came to see them reveal the truth of one of sport's most enduring equations — that while sport builds character on the one side it reveals it on the other. A decade before the U.S. Olympic Women's Hockey Team found gold on Mt. Olympus, before the U.S. National Soccer Team's Brandi Chastain scored on an overtime penalty kick against China to bring the Women's World Cup to the Girls of Summer, before the WNBA proved conclusively that "she got game," I watched a generation of girls and young women reveal a physical durability and mental strength that matches or exceeds anything I saw in years of writing about professional sports for a living. I've seen women return to play after taking shots in the face, after trips to the hospital, stitches in the chin and sticks across the hands. I saw a player sustain a broken nose and return for the next game wearing a fiberglass goalie mask of the sort now seen only in horror movies.

But the day I remember best is an afternoon in Tracey's senior year when two varsity football players on their way back to the gym from football practice — both linemen judging from their jersey numbers, 63 and 78 — stopped and sat on their helmets while watching the last few minutes of a varsity field hockey game. After about five minutes of watching girls swing thick wooden sticks to send a rock-hard ball toward other girls whose only protective equipment was a mouthpiece and low shin guards, one lineman turned and said to the other, "You've got to be [bleeping] crazy to play this game."

I also saw something by watching Tracey emerge from her mother's hockey shadow. When Tracey was voted a first-team Bay State League All-Star — an honor that had eluded her mother — I knew she'd done it on her own terms. Where Barbara, according to her sisters, had played with crash-the-net abandon, Tracey's game, on the field as on the ice, was one of quick transition and seeing-eye passes. Then, as now, Barbara wants to leave a trail of bodies; Tracey has an almost Gretzkian preoccupation with the creation and exploitation of space. And aren't these styles perfect metaphors for their respective athletic generations? Barbara taking what she needs; Tracey using what you give her.

(One of the minor disappointments of my sporting life was the cancellation of a mother-daughter game tentatively scheduled during Tracey's sophomore year on a high school team where several of the girls' mothers had played high school or college field hockey. The game was called off when there weren't enough moms to field a team. But, had it been played, it would have matched Barbara, a center forward, against Tracey, a center midfielder, in head-to-head competition. Elegance and imagination vs. unbending will. My money was on unbending will. "The scalpers could get a hundred dollars ringside for that one," said Brian. "They'll kill each other.")

Tracey is married now and has a child of her own, so my days of watching her play are over. But I still remember all that those days revealed, including the revelation that I — and any parent watching a son or daughter play — must find unsettling.

As I watched those field hockey games from late August to early November, I noticed the shadows creeping across the field a little earlier each game. I felt it get colder. The golf shirt and walking shorts I wore in September gave way to sweat pants and a down parka by October. It was on one of those cold, late-October afternoons in Tracey's senior year that I finally got the answer to her then-four-year-old question.

I had taken one of the apples out of the bag, eaten it and carelessly tossed the core toward a fence where it lay in a ray of heatless sunlight. There a wasp — a yellow jacket no doubt drawn to the apple for its sugar — lighted on it. As I watched that wasp crawl upon that browning apple core, I saw the full answer to my daughter's question.

What was I doing at those games? Like most parents at most games — and like that wasp — I was instinctively seeking the last sweetness of autumn before the shadows and the cold and the night beyond.

Building a Rink of Your Own

I don't understand the exact triggering mechanism, but I get the urge for digging every October when low gray clouds come scudding in on a northwest wind, the frost-blackened tomato plants hang limp on their hockey stick poles and the leaves of our two maple trees turn red and orange in that final leap of arboreal flame as summer burns itself out before the relentless advance of the long, dark New England winter.

That said, there is nothing especially lyrical about digging twenty-three postholes while trying to angle the northeast corner of the rink around the southeast corner of an abandoned septic tank, the concrete cover of which will not permit posthole digging. It does, however, make a very interesting configuration in that corner of our rink, where a sideboard suddenly juts out at about a thirty-five-degree angle, a board I credit with teaching a generation of young hockey players the game's oldest rule — keep your head up.

But before we go too far with the digging, nailing and flooding, let me make a couple of disclaimers:

What I'm about to describe is not the *only* way to build a rink. It probably isn't even the best way. Indeed, there are as many ways of building a backyard rink as there are rink owners. But this is the way that has worked for me for seventeen years. If you can improve on it — and you probably can — I wish you well. As for me? I'm going to stick with what I know works.

The Basic Idea

Our backyard rink is essentially a corral of plywood boards lined with a sheet of plastic and filled with water to an average depth of roughly ten inches (i.e. four or five inches at the shallow end and fourteen to sixteen inches at the deep end). To this we've added a few features like screening above the boards to keep the pucks in play, floodlights, a real hockey net, flags of various hockey-playing nations and our own banner — a custom-made flag with our rink's name in red letters on a white background: *The Bacon Street Omni.*

I know of a few people — Wayne Gretzky's father Walter among them — who simply flooded natural depressions in their yards and, aided by deeply frozen ground or tamped-down snow, were able to create a rink without using a plastic liner. But if you live south of Canada or the USA's northern tier states you're better off using plastic to keep the water from seeping into the ground or leaking away during what, in recent years, have been all too many mid-winter warming spells.

One caveat: Don't try building a rink unless you have a relatively flat backyard. We have about a one-foot variance from the highest to the lowest points in our yard. What's the maximum variance you can get away with? I don't think any-one can say with certainty but my best estimate — based on the way the water pressure bends our plywood boards — is in the vicinity of sixteen inches.

Building Materials

Your main start-up cost will be for plywood, studs and plastic. You can build a rink without any power tools. A posthole digger or an auger would help, but I still dig my postholes with a long-handled garden spade and a spud (see below) and that works just fine. A saw, a claw ham-mer and a staple gun will be the only other tools you should need.

I made my rink boards by buying fourteen sheets of four-by-eight-foot three-quarter-inch plywood. I then had the building supply store cut seven of the boards in half length-wise, thus giving me fourteen two-by-eight-foot boards in addition to the other seven uncut four-by-eight boards. I use the big boards at the deep end, or what we call the "shoot-ing end," of the rink and the low boards around the rest of the rink. If you plan to play hockey end-to-end — instead of the kind of "half-court" game we play — then obviously you'd want high boards at both ends of the rink.

You'll also need about thirty ten-foot studs. Twenty-one of those studs will serve as the "legs" of the large boards. I nail one stud at each end and one in the middle of each four-by-eight sheet of plywood so that two feet of the stud extend below the board (this will be the leg that goes into the ground) and four feet extend above the board (I later nail garden wire to these studs to keep pucks from flying out of the rink).

Cut the remaining studs into three-foot lengths (you'll get three from each stud) to be used as the legs on the low boards. I use one leg at each end of the low boards, nailing the stud so that its top is flush with the top of the board, and the one foot of stud extending below the board is the leg that will go into the ground to hold the board in place.

The boards will be a one-time expense and a one-time labor. We still have a few boards from our first rink built in 1982, and even the ones that we had to replace lasted at least eight to ten years. It's also a lot easier to replace one or two boards each season than to build all of them from scratch.

For my plastic liner I buy a seamless sheet of six-mil clear plastic in a standard size of forty feet wide and one hundred feet long. That forty-foot width is commonly available, although I recently learned it is possible to order sixty-foot-wide sheets. Assuming you use the typical forty-foot-wide sheet, you won't want your rink to be more than about thirty-five feet wide at its widest point because you'll need the extra five feet of plastic to extend up the boards to hold in the water.

The plastic is, for me, an annual expense because it gets ripped from skates, pucks, shovels and the industrial staples that hold it to the boards. I get clear plastic instead of the easier-to-find green because the darker color will absorb more heat from the sun and that's something I don't want.

A tip: I skip what would otherwise be the final lawn mowing of the year in my backyard. I like to let the grass grow long to serve as a natural cushion for the plastic and to protect it from sharp pebbles or old staples or whatever else might puncture the liner. Likewise, I'm happy to let a few autumn leaves build up where the boards go into the ground. These also serve as a natural cushion (but it's a miserable job to rake them out in the spring when they're waterlogged and half-rotted).

Can You Dig It?

The hardest part of building a rink is digging the postholes and putting up the boards. You've got to get this done before the ground freezes, which here in southern New England can be late November to mid-December. My target date for having all the boards in place is Thanksgiving, and I haven't been frozen out yet.

The holes for the big boards are about two feet deep and the holes for the lower boards are a little more than one foot deep. By now I've dug through the same ground so often that the soil is cleared of heavy rocks and the job gets easier from year to year. On the other hand, posthole digging is unpleasant work, so I make it palatable by doing it in short bursts. Indeed, I can — and often do —dig a two-foot-deep hole during halftime of an NFL or NCAA football telecast. And before Daylight Savings Time ends I'll often use the late afternoon to get a little exercise by digging a hole and putting a board in place.

If your soil is especially rocky you may want to get a spud — a four-foot metal rod with a chisel-like point — to serve as a kind of pick axe, loosening the soil and making it easy to shovel. A hatchet or small saw is also useful if you have to cut through tree roots. *A tip:* Pile up the dirt *behind* the hole (i.e., outside of the skating area) so sharp pebbles that bury themselves in the grass won't pose a threat to your plastic liner.

Obviously, one posthole can accommodate two board legs. The ends of each board should be touching each other to create the smoothest seam possible. Not every seam will be perfect (we'll deal with that problem in a few more paragraphs) but you want the boards as close together as you can get them.

As you lower each board into its hole and refill the hole with dirt, make sure you tamp down the ground firmly to hold the board in place.

There are probably easier ways to do this. A friend of mine who is in the building trades and is far more adept with power tools than I am has affixed three-quarter-inch pipe as legs on his low boards and has sunk one-inch pipes into the ground to serve as sleeves. He can pop his low boards into place in a few minutes. And when he removes them in the spring he simply caps the tops of the pipes that remain in the ground. However, the system doesn't work as well on the larger boards and for those he uses the same system I use.

Sealing the Seams

When all the boards are in place you will have completed your "corral." But because the seams — the places where two boards meet — rarely will be perfectly flush, you'll want to cover them with a soft, strong material to prevent the plastic from ripping on the rough, sometimes splintery end of a board or from being pushed out through a gap in the boards and rupturing under the accumulating pressure of the water. At various times I've used canvas from an old tent, strips of carpeting, pieces of artificial turf and strips cut from an old leather jacket. I secure the strips over the seams with five-eighths-inch tacks. If I have a large opening — say anything more than a half inch — at the deep end of the rink I sometimes nail a piece of wood over the gap and then cover the wood with a soft fabric.

Besides sealing the vertical seams you also have to pay attention to the horizontal seams — the places where the bottoms of boards meet the ground. Since your yard is probably uneven, there will be gaps where the bottom of a board is not perfectly flush with the ground. I fill these gaps with old sheets or rags collectively known in our house as "rink rags." About a dozen times in the course of a year Barbara will hold up an old coat or curtain or blanket she plans on throwing out and ask, "You want this for a rink rag?" The answer is invariably yes.

Put the rink rags inside the boards where they will also help to cushion the plastic liner and prevent it from being pushed out under the boards by the pressure of the water.

Warning: Don't install the plastic liner until the day you're ready to flood. The longer the plastic is exposed the greater the danger it will get torn. And even if it doesn't get torn it will collect leaves, most of which will rise to the top when you flood, thus temporarily ruining the ice surface.

Fence Me In

When the boards are in place I nail a long strip of garden wire (*Note:* Chicken wire isn't strong enough to stop a puck unless your shot's even weaker than mine) to the studs above the high boards on the "shooting end" of the rink, thus raising the total height of the backstop (boards and fencing combined) to about seven feet, high enough to keep most shots from sailing out of the rink. In recent years I've taken to nailing the heavier garden fencing to the inside of the studs, then nailing a roll of chicken wire to the outside of the studs, thus giving me a double wall of fencing inches apart. What happens is that a hard shot (hey, don't look at me) that forces its way through the inner garden wire will have lost all of its power by the time it hits the chicken wire and, thus, will drop straight to the ground inches behind the boards. Pucks are a lot easier to recover when they're all in the same place instead of sprayed all over the yard. We call this the Bacon Street Omni Automatic Puck Recovery System. But we haven't patented it so you can use it.

Flooding

Timing is everything when it comes to flooding. Don't get fooled by those first few frosty days of late fall or early winter. What you need is about a three-day stretch of serious cold wherein night temperatures drop to the teens or single digits on the Fahrenheit scale and daytime temperatures don't rise above freezing. The colder the better.

But you also want to flood a day *ahead* of an arriving cold front. In December I become the Weather Channel's biggest fan as I watch for a sustained blast of cold Canadian air slamming down out of Alberta and heading for New England. Approximately twelve to twenty-four hours before the cold front's arrival I'm ready to put in the plastic liner and start flooding.

Rolling out the Plastic

Roll out your plastic and staple it to the sides of your rink boards. Make sure the plastic liner extends far enough up the boards to be above the water level. We staple ours all the way up on the low boards and about three feet high on the high boards. You can always trim away extra plastic, but if the water rises so high that it flows out of the rink you've got trouble.

As soon as the plastic is in place, turn on the hose and start flooding. Using one standard garden hose it takes us between eighteen and twenty-six hours to fill our rink. If your outdoor faucet is frozen — and if it isn't frozen on the day you flood you can be sure it will be during the heart of the skating season — simply pour warm water on it. Even on the coldest day, two saucepans of warm water will thaw out a faucet.

Check your rink frequently while you're flooding. The rising water exerts so much pressure on the plastic that it often pulls it off of the boards, in which case you have to go out and re-staple. It's easy to re-staple the plastic to the low boards, but the high boards — the place where our plastic is most likely to pull away — are another matter. Twice I've had to wade out in frigid water to restaple the plastic. But that was before I figured out that if I left the wire fencing loose at the bottom I'd have enough room to reach under the fencing and over the boards to restaple. Once we have ice — and before the pucks start flying around — I take a few finish nails and complete the fastening of the fencing.

You also want to keep an eye on all of your seams — vertical and horizontal — to make sure there's no leakage. Even at night I go out with a flashlight every three or four hours, checking for problems. You won't get much sleep on the night of the first flooding.

Making Ice

Ice makes itself, so this is the easy part.

When you think you have enough water in the rink — as a rough guide I'd say you want at least three inches at the shallowest point — simply put the hose back in the cellar (it will freeze if you don't) and wait for Nature to do its winter's work. But wait patiently.

The water will skim over quickly — usually while the hose is still running — but it could be two to four days, or even longer, before your ice is thick enough to skate on.

I have a series of tests for my ice, beginning with a few taps on the surface with the blade of a hockey stick. If the ice can withstand that, then I usually butt-end it with the stick, the resulting hole giving me a good idea of the thickness of the ice.

When I can't drive the butt end of the hockey stick through the ice, then I step over the low boards and — holding onto the board — I gradually transfer my weight onto the ice until I hear a crack. If the ice doesn't crack, then I put my entire weight on it and shuffle around a little bit. If the ice cracks I get off it immediately. But if I can walk around the entire rink without hearing any ominous crackings then I can be fairly certain that the ice is ready for skating.

Warning: Don't go checking the thickness of your ice while wearing skates. If you should break through the ice the blade of the skate will probably rip your plastic liner and, to the best of my knowledge, that's an impossible repair job.

Resurfacing

Thou shalt not skate if thou hast not shoveled. That's the first commandment of rink ownership as it applies to any skater ten years old or older. A backyard rink is a lot of fun, but first you have to pay your dues.

After the rink has been skated on for a while, snow will begin to build up to a point where it interferes with stick-handling and passing the puck, and if it builds up deep enough, it will interfere with skating. If you're not through skating for the day then all you have to do is scrape the snow off the ice and keep on playing. We scrape our ice with plastic shovels, which seem to do a better job and to snag on the ice less than aluminum ones, though I don't know why that is.

Do not put water on the ice if you plan to use the rink again that day. It is amazing how long it takes a sprayed rink to freeze up, especially when compared to the almost instant freezing you see when a machine resurfaces an indoor rink. But even when outdoor temperatures have been in the teens and twenties I've made the mistake of trying to resurface the ice only to have to wait hours — sometimes half a day — before the ice is ready to skate on.

But when you're finished with the rink for the day, then you'll want to resurface it completely. Here's how:

1. Take the goal off the rink. We slide ours over to the low sideboards and simply tip it upside-down and out of the rink so that the crossbar is lying on the ground. It's easy to tilt it back the next day. If you leave the goal — especially a metal-framed goal — on the ice, the water you put down will build up around the goal frame and will freeze the goal into the ice, a dangerous situation if and when someone crashes into the goal post. Also, a warm, sunny day during a mid-winter thaw will see the goalposts warm up and melt their way into the ice, again making the goal immovable and dangerous for any player who crashes into it.

2. Scrape the rink. I said that when I reached fifty years of age I'd buy a snowblower for the rink, but as I write this, I'm fifty-five and I still clear the ice with a plastic shovel. I rationalize this as having some cardiovascular benefit, though I think there might be some macho taint to my thought process.

3. Drag out the hose and begin spraying. I start at the high boards and work from sideboard to sideboard back toward the shallow end, where I step over the low boards and am standing outside of the rink when I spray the last few square feet of ice.

4. Throw the hose back in the cellar and have a good night's sleep. Your ice will be as good as new in the morning.

Tip: Have both ends of the hose facing **up** when carrying the hose to the cellar or bulkhead. If either end is facing down, water can run onto your porch or your bulkhead steps, freeze and present a safety hazard. I try to drain out most of the water when I disconnect the hose, but I don't mind if a quart or so stays in the hose and runs out on my cellar floor. Better there, where it will evaporate quickly, than on the porch or stairs where it might stay frozen for weeks.

Lights

Floodlights will let you get added hours of enjoyment from your rink. We have four 150-watt adjustable flood lights mounted on a garage beside the rink and another mounted on the porch roof. Together they light up almost the entire ice surface and allow us to skate at night. Just make sure the lights are far enough away from the rink so that they won't be hit by a deflected puck.

And one word of warning about night hockey. We have what we call a "Six O'clock Rule" which says that after six o'clock at night, all hockey will be played with tennis balls, not pucks. This is to keep the noise down and not intrude upon neighbors.

Taking Down Your Rink

Sometime between Valentine's Day at the earliest and St. Patrick's Day at the latest a rising sun and gradually warming temperatures will begin melting our ice and evaporating some of the water, thus rendering the rink unusable. It's obvious when it's time to drain the rink and store the boards. It's not my favorite job, but as the years go on, it's become part of the ritual of spring—which is to say I deal with it better when I think of rink removal less as the end of the skating season and more as the earliest harbinger of summer.

Drain it Slowly

When the ice in the north or shallow end begins to melt, I use a dandelion picker to poke holes in the plastic. But be careful. If your rink is near your house — as ours is — you don't want to poke so many holes that the escaping water saturates the ground and floods your cellar. I got greedy one year and jabbed about fifty holes in the plastic liner. Six hours later I had the beginnings of an indoor swimming pool in my cellar. Now I poke ten or a dozen holes in the shallowest part of the rink and when the water recedes, I step out onto the plastic and poke a dozen more holes. The effect is like the tide going out on a plastic beach.

When the plastic is exposed I take a pair of shears and cut it sideways (that is along its forty-foot width) into strips roughly four to six feet wide. Then I fold each strip in half lengthwise, roll it up and tie it with a string preparatory to stacking it up like so much plastic cordwood to await the arrival of the trash collectors or a trip to the dump.

After the plastic is out, I take a claw hammer and pull the tacks out of all the strips of fabric that I used to seal the vertical seams. Be careful removing these tacks. You don't want to lose one in the grass where it could pierce your liner next year, or worse, someone could step on it. I save these pieces of fabric and reuse them from year to year.

I then take down the fencing and transfer it immediately into the garden where it does summer duty as a trellis for peas.

It's easy to pull out the low boards and store them in the garage. But the big boards — the four-by-eight-footers with the ten-foot studs nailed to them — are another and more difficult matter. Removing them is a two-person job. We use two long-handled shovels as levers. Run the blade of the shovel under the board, then step on the handle and the board will begin to come out of the ground, whereupon you and your partner can lift it out completely and carry it to its summer storage area, which in our case is against the back and sides of our garage.

Fill in the postholes and throw some grass seed on the dirt around them. After a few mowings you'll hardly be able to see where your rink has been.

One of the questions I've been asked most frequently is: Doesn't the rink kill the grass? No. The plastic liner actually serves as a kind of greenhouse so that the grass that has been under the plastic (and under the ice) usually begins to turn green before the grass in the rest of the yard.

I'm not going to sugarcoat it. Building and maintaining a rink is hard work in cold weather. But worth it? It is when I go out for an early morning skate, when Barbara, leaving the rink lights off, skates beneath a spray of winter stars, and when, in winters past, we watched our children and their friends lose themselves in the joy of impromptu hockey games. In two or three years we hope to see our first grand-child — born a few weeks before this chapter was written — take his first wobbly skating strides here at the Bacon Street Omni.

Worth it? As Barbara said: "Anyone can love summer, but to love winter you have to carry your sunshine around with you."

Our rink lights up our life.

Last Skate

I hadn't seen the pond in more than forty years, and saw it this time only because I had to drive past it on my way to visit an aunt in the hospital. I remembered it as such a tiny, shallow pond that I didn't even know it still existed, much less had a name. But there it was just a few yards into the woods on the west side of South Border Road in Medford, Massachusetts. "Bellevue Pond," read the sign in front of a small paved parking lot — a place where old men sat in cars and read newspapers — behind which sat the pond itself, as small as I'd remembered it. You could hit a pitching wedge across it. It was the first place I'd skated.

It was school vacation week between Christmas and New Year's and my mother and aunt — my mother's older sister — had taken my younger sister Elizabeth and me to the pond to try out the skates we'd received from a Santa Claus we still wanted to — but didn't — believe in.

My skates were cheap ones without much padding in the tongue and with a boot that offered a chafing stiffness but little support or comfort. I forget what off-brand they were, but it's safe to say they weren't Tacks, which in those days were known by their full name: Tackaberrys. Of course I didn't know then that my skates weren't good ones and neither did my parents, and even if they did, I doubt they could have afforded Tacks.

My mother helped me into the skates — to this day I have not figured out a comfortable way to put on my skates while kneeling on a frozen pond — and I went tottering ahead gingerly and with much waving of my arms. The only clear memory I have of those first few strides is of the contrast between the blackness of the ice and the stark white of the cuts made by the blades of other skaters. Natural ice did not look like the ice I'd seen in Currier and Ives lithographs. The feeling I had was one of vulnerability as other, older and better skaters whizzed around me.

My mother must have sensed my insecurity, because when she came out onto the ice wearing an old pair of figure skates, the once-white boots of which looked like they'd been dyed in tea, she stood a few feet away, held out her arms and encouraged me to skate toward her. It was the same strategy she used in teaching me to swim: stay close, present a reachable goal, make no reference to anyone or anything else, and reward the achievement with a few kind words. It's a strategy I use today when I teach a college writing class.

I remember stumbling toward her and half crashing, half throwing myself into her outstretched arms, and then pressing and being pressed into the warmth and softness of her fake fur coat. I did that a few times before I developed the ability and willingness to go shuffling around on my own. I don't remember how long we skated, but it must have been until deep into the afternoon, because the light had changed and the pond that was in sunlight when we arrived was in the long shadows of bare trees when we left. I hadn't known it was so late.

That was the first and only time my sister and I skated with my mother. It was also the last time my mother skated. A few months later, pregnant, she was diagnosed with cancer. And several months after that she and the son to whom she had prematurely given birth, Stephen Charles, were dead.

Driving past that pond and recalling that day I skated with my mother, I thought how good it is that we cannot see beyond the present. I also thought how skating and hockey helped me through the dark decade after my mother's death. That what she had set in motion that day on the pond would remain in motion until today, when I have a wife, children, grandchild, home and a small homemade skating pond of my own.

I would become an adequate skater, though never a fast one, and never good enough to please myself. I think this is why even today when I'm alone on the rink, I follow a ritual I designed to improve my skating, or at the very least to fight a rearguard action against age making me worse. Before I tilt the net over the low boards and push it to its place in front of the high boards, before I start fooling around with a puck, I go through my warmup routine: without the puck I skate five laps clockwise, five counterclockwise, five figure eights, two laps backward clockwise and two counterclockwise. I used to skate three backward laps in each direction but found that I sometimes got dizzy and fell over backward, which gave me a good chance of whacking my unhelmeted head on the ice and also raised the existential question: *If a skater falls and no one sees him is he still embarrassed?* Yes, he is.

I then stickhandle with the puck three laps clockwise, three counterclockwise. If I lose the puck I have to start over. That done, I feel free to have fun, which for me consists mainly of cruising around the rink trying to shoot pucks into the corners of the net, often from bad angles. My favorite shot is a backhander from the right wing into the top left corner. I love it when the puck clinks in off the post or the crossbar — love it so much I sometimes raise my stick in the air just as if the goal meant something, which to me it does. My feeling must be like that of the fly fisherman who practice casts for the sheer joy and beauty of the act, though I can't imagine fly fishermen pumping their casting arms in the air after a particularly elegant presentation. Different culture. Fly fishing is a zen pleasure. Hockey is a blood sport. Though I suppose fly fishing is a blood sport if you're a fish.

After I've had my fill of shooting — or have shot all the pucks out of the rink, whichever comes first — I do a few stops and starts, skating the length of the rink and hitting the brakes near the boards, then digging back the other way. I don't push very hard. Just enough to break a sweat and keep the heart rate up. Then it's a couple of easy warm-down laps before I step over the low boards, waddle down the plywood walkway and clump into the kitchen, there to collapse into a chair and take off my skates, scraping the snow off the blades with my hand and tossing the little ice ball into the sink. Except when I toss it at someone, usually Barbara. How old do you have to be before you stop throwing skate snow at people? Older than fifty-five, I guess.

As January pushes into February and the sun, daily rising toward the vernal equinox, hits the ice at ever higher angles, I can't help wondering which skating session will be my last for that season. Even on the coldest late February days the midday sun reflecting off of the south-facing boards will soften and often melt the ice at that end of the rink. I think it was this curiosity about what would be the final skating day of the season that led Barbara and me to start recording the season's last skate in our rink's guest book.

I bought the leather-bound, gold-embossed guest book in 1989. Originally we used it to record the date of the season's first skate and the name of each person skating on the rink for the first time in a given winter. "Signing in" was part of the ritual of skating at the Bacon Street Omni. For the first few years guests merely signed their name and address and the date of their first skate. But beginning in 1996 some skaters began recording spontaneous comments:

2/3/96 Ashley and Don . . . "We love the rink, the chili and the company."

1/19/97 David Reynolds . . . "First skate. How am I doing, Ma?" [written by his father]

2/4/97 Chris Smith . . . "Let's see Dale Earnhardt negotiate the Omni corners."

1/29/00 Beth Smith . . . "seven months pregnant."

Then, six winters ago, Barbara and I began noting the date of each season's final skate even though we had to do so days after the fact because with natural ice you never truly know what skate will be the final one. But in late February and early March I often get a feeling similar to the one I get when Barbara and I walk off the beach on Cape Cod on the last weekend in August. I just know in my bones that we won't be back again that year. I cover it up with a lot of talk about how September is the best month on New England's beaches and about how we live so close to the Cape we can zip down to the beach any time we want to. But summer's over and I know it. It's just too sad to say it out loud.

As I look in our guest book I see that I have taken the final skate in three of the six seasons we've been keeping that record. Twice by myself. Once with Barbara. And all three times I knew intuitively that it would be the final skate. And even when I wasn't the last skater off the ice in a given season, I still knew when I was taking my own last skate, and on those days I stayed out longer and skated harder. Of course I didn't skate any better, I just did what I've tried to do ever since I took those first shuffling strides with my mother — skate as well as I can. Because life is different from a skating season, and in life you never know which skate will be your last. Only that one of them will be.

Acknowledgments

Because a writer works alone doesn't mean his goals go unassisted. I could not — and would not — have written and published *Home Ice* without the help and encouragement of several people, most notably my wife and occasional right wing, Barbara. It was she who, in the summer of 1999, pressed me to begin writing this book, suggesting that instead of waiting for the Muse to visit I should get myself to the writing desk and there the Muse would find me. She was right. Without Barbara there would be no book.

I also want to thank Lonnie Herman of McGregor Publishing who, acting only on the basis of having read four of these essays, was willing to take a chance on a book that doesn't fit neatly into any pre-existing niche. It was a gutsy call. Then he did something I especially appreciate but which publishers and editors are often loath to do — he left me alone while I wrote the book.

And my thanks to Bobby Orr for a big assist (let's see, that would be the 712th assist of his career, counting playoffs) with his heartfelt foreword and his inspiring, undiminished and obvious love for a game he played better than it has ever been played.

Steve Dryden, Editor-in-Chief of *The Hockey News* and its former sister publication *Inside Hockey* magazine, in which four of these chapters were originally published — albeit in slightly different form — assisted by letting me, indeed often encouraging me, to float up near the blue line of whimsy and introspection even though his more pressing journalistic need was undoubtedly for more muckers and grinders bang-ing along the reportorial walls.

Sixteen years ago my artist friend Steve Lockwood gave me the watercolor — originally entitled "Making Ice. The Hoser" — that now adorns the cover of this book and that, I think, captures the warmth and homey feeling of the back-yard rink. My thanks to Steve and to cover designer Bob Antler, Antler Designworks, for selecting that painting.

My son and daughter, Brian and Tracey, not only encour-aged me to write *Home Ice* but also unwittingly and togeth-er with their friends provided many of the quotes and anec-dotes that appear in these essays. They seem to have an almost inbred understanding of the worth and meaning of the rink as shown annually by the hours they've spent shov-eling, resurfacing and helping with the boards. Thanks, guys. And I'll buy a snowblower one of these days. Really. Honest.

Thanks also to copyeditor Sue Knopf, my ally in the comma wars and a careful reader who, in editing my manu-script, probably made more saves than goalie Patrick Roy.

And though I can't truly thank him in the literal sense, I want to acknowledge the contribution of my friend Gerry Sisto. It was Gerry who came up with a workable design for my rink and who badgered me relentlessly to write this book. Gerry died in the summer of 1999, exactly one week before I received the contract to write *Home Ice.*

JACK FALLA
NATICK, MASSACHUSETTS